BEGINNER

Helen Stephenson

Paul Dummett

John Hughes

Contents

Pronunciation	Listening	Reading	Speaking	Writing
word stress questions	introductions	a description of two people in the Himalayas an article about phone calls from New York	personal information a quiz phone numbers	text type: an identity badge writing skill: capital letters (1)
we're, they're *isn't, aren't* *be* questions and short answers plural nouns syllables	a description of a place a conversation on holiday	a blog about a holiday a quiz about holiday places	holiday photos on holiday general knowledge	text type: a form writing skill: capital letters (2)
possessive *'s* linking with *at* exclamations	information about a family from India a description of the Cousteau family	a description of a wedding in Thailand an article about age pyramids in different countries	your family tree a wedding your family pyramid	text type: a greetings card writing skill: contractions
th /ð/ linking with *can*	a description of Shanghai at a tourist information centre	information about a town centre a description of two famous towers an article about times around the world	locations famous places times and timetables	text type: a postcard writing skill: *and*
can/can't numbers	information about Yves Rossy an interview with a robot expert	an article about a robot a blog about technology an article about cooking with the sun	your abilities your favourite object buy online	text type: an email writing skill: *but*
do you … ? *likes, doesn't like* intonation	information about football and the World Cup an interview with a man about his likes and dislikes	an article about giant vegetables a profile of a TV presenter an article about racing with animals	a food survey things in common a sports event	text type: a review writing skill: pronouns

Pronunciation	Listening	Reading	Speaking	Writing
don't intonation in questions sentence stress	information about the Holi festival an interview with a teacher an interview with a student	an article about traditional life an article about the seasons of the year	you and your partner a survey activities in different seasons	text type: a profile writing skill: paragraphs
-s and *-es* verbs /s/ and /z/	an interview with a man about his job a description of a writer's daily routine a conversation about a *National Geographic* explorer	an article about a typical day an article about a job in tiger conservation	routines your friends and family a quiz	text type: an email writing skill: spelling: double letters
there are *I'd like*	four people talking about travel a conversation in which two people plan a trip	an article about things in your suitcase an article about a Trans-Siberia trip	things in your suitcase hotel rooms travel tips	text type: travel advice writing skill: *because*
was/were weak forms strong forms sentence stress	information about an important moment in TV history a radio programme about heroes	a quiz about 'firsts' in exploration an article about the first people in the American continents	dates and events people in the past famous Americans	text type: a blog writing skill: *when*
-ed verbs *did you … ?* *didn't*	information about discoveries in Papua New Guinea a story about the investigation of a discovery an interview about discovering your local area	an article about an unusual discovery an interview with an adventurer an article about an accident in Madagascar	your family's past what did you do last year? telling a story	text type: an email writing skill: expressions in emails
going and *doing* *would you … ?*	information about the weekend in different countries a description of a family in Indonesia a conversation between two friends about this weekend	an article about helping people at the weekend	your photos next weekend a special weekend	text type: an invitation writing skill: spelling: verb endings

Life around the world

Unit 4 Where's that?

A video quiz about four cities.

Unit 5 What's your favourite gadget?

People talk about their favourite gadget.

Norv

UK

USA

Unit 6 At the market

Meet people at a market in an English city.

Unit 10 The space race

What was the 'space race'? Find out in this video.

São Tomé and Príncipe

Unit 12 Saturday morning in São Tomé

Meet some local artists in this small African country.

Bolivia

Unit 2 Antarctica

Holidays in Antarctica.

Unit 9 Along the Inca Road

Discover South America with writer Karin Muller.

Antarctica

Unit 7 The people of the reindeer

Life with the Sami people in Scandinavia.

Unit 3 A Mongolian family

Meet a family in Mongolia.

Mongolia

Nepal

Unit 1 My top ten photos

A photographer talks about his favourite photos.

Unit 8 The elephants of Samburu

Meet a man who photographs elephants.

Kenya

Madagascar

Unit 11 Perfumes from Madagascar

Why do scientists love Madagascar?

UNIT 1
HELLO

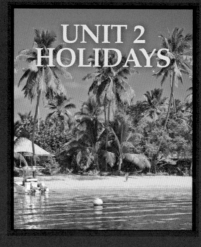

UNIT 2
HOLIDAYS

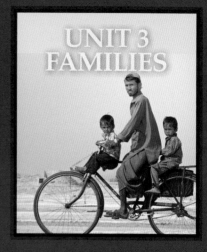

UNIT 3
FAMILIES

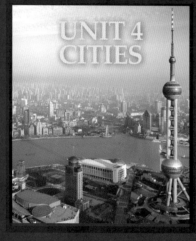

UNIT 4
CITIES

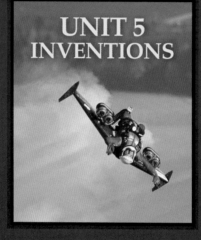

UNIT 5
INVENTIONS

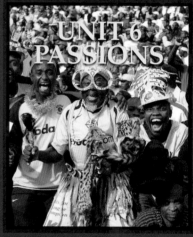

UNIT 6
PASSIONS

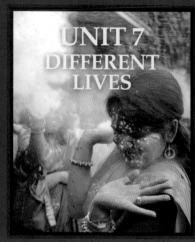

UNIT 7
DIFFERENT LIVES

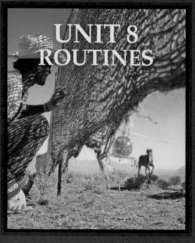

UNIT 8
ROUTINES

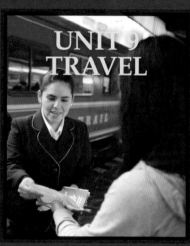

UNIT 9
TRAVEL

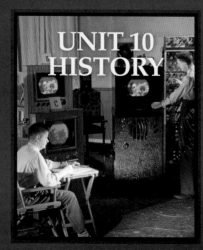

UNIT 10
HISTORY

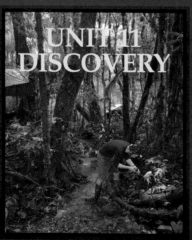

UNIT 11
DISCOVERY

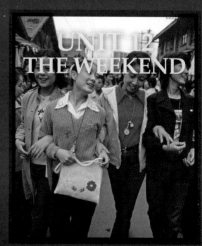

UNIT 12
THE WEEKEND

Pacific Ocean, Australia
Photo by David Doubilet

FEATURES

1 1.1 Look at the photo. Listen and tick (✓).

a Hi! My name's Mike.
b Hello! I'm Mike.
c Hi! I'm Mike.

2 1.1 Listen and repeat.

3 Write your name.

Hi! I'm _____ .

4 Work in pairs.

Hello! I'm Meera.

Hi! My name's Jared.

1a *National Geographic* people

Vocabulary **jobs**

1 🎵 **1.2** Look at the photos. Listen to the people.

Hi. I'm Mattias. I'm a filmmaker.

2 🎵 **1.3** Listen and repeat the jobs.

> explorer   filmmaker
> photographer   scientist   writer

3 Look at the photos. Write the jobs.

1 Hi. I'm Carolyn. I'm a _____ .
2 Hello. I'm Alex. I'm a _____ .
3 Hi. I'm Mireya. I'm a _____ .
4 Hi. I'm Mattias. I'm a _____ .
5 Hello. I'm Robert. I'm an _____ .

4 Complete the sentence with your job.

I'm _____ .

5 Talk to four people in your class.

> *Hi. I'm Katya. I'm a student.*

N A T I O N A L   G E O G R A P H I C   P E O P L E

Mattias Klum in Malaysia

Mattias Klum
filmmaker

Carolyn Anderson
writer

Robert Ballard
explorer

Mireya Mayor
scientist

Alex Treadway
photographer

Grammar *a/an*

6 Look at the grammar box and the example. Then look at the jobs in Exercise 2. Underline the first letter.

Example: <u>e</u>xplorer

A	AN
a + noun with *b, c, d, f, …* *a filmmaker*	an + noun with *a, e, i, o, u* *an explorer*
For further information and practice, see page 161.	

7 🔊 1.4 Complete the sentences with *a* or *an*. Then listen, check and repeat the sentences.

 1    2

 3   4

 5    6

1   I'm *a* photographer.
2   I'm   doctor.
3   I'm   teacher.
4   I'm   artist.
5   I'm   engineer.
6   I'm   driver.

Listening

8 🔊 1.5 Listen to a conversation. Put the conversation in order. Then listen again and check.

a   Yes.
b   Oh, you're a photographer!
c   Hello.   *1*
d   I'm Alex Treadway.
e   Hi.

9 🔊 1.6 Listen and complete the conversation.

You're   I'm   Hi   Hello

YOU: ¹ ....
MATTIAS: ² .... ³ .... Mattias Klum.
YOU: Oh, ⁴ .... a filmmaker!
MATTIAS: Yes, for *National Geographic*.

Grammar *I + am, you + are*

▶ *I + AM, YOU + ARE*	
I'm	Katya.
You're	a student.
(I'm = I am, You're = You are)	
For further information and practice, see page 161.	

10 Work in pairs. Look at the photos on page 10. Practise the conversations in Exercises 8 and 9.

11 Work in groups. Play a game.

Student A: Act a job.

Students B, C, D: Say the job.

Take turns.

Vocabulary **the alphabet**

12 🔊 1.7 Listen and repeat the alphabet.

Aa	Bb	Cc	Dd	Ee	Ff	Gg
Hh	Ii	Jj	Kk	Ll	Mm	
Nn	Oo	Pp	Qq	Rr	Ss	Tt
Uu	Vv	Ww	Xx	Yy	Zz	

13 🔊 1.7 Say these letters. Then listen again. Complete the table.

A	B	F	I	O	Q	R
H	C	L				
	D					

14 🔊 1.8 Listen and choose the correct name.
1   Paula / Paola   3   Shaun / Sean
2   Bryan / Brian   4   Anna / Ana

15 Work in pairs. Spell your name.

16 Work in pairs. Spell words.

Student A: Turn to page 153.

Student B: Turn to page 157.

Speaking

17 Work in groups. Play a memory game. Introduce yourself. Then give information about other people.

> I'm Katya.
> I'm a student.

> You're Katya. You're a student.
> You're Paola. You're a doctor.

1b People and places

Reading

1 Read the article. Complete the table.

	Photo 1	Photo 2
Name	Manu	
Country		
Nationality		Indian

2 🔊 **1.9** Listen and check your answers.

PEOPLE AND PLACES BY ALEX TREADWAY

Alex Treadway is a British photographer with *National Geographic*.

1 This is Manu. He's from Jagat. Jagat is in Nepal. Manu is Nepalese.
Photo by Alex Treadway

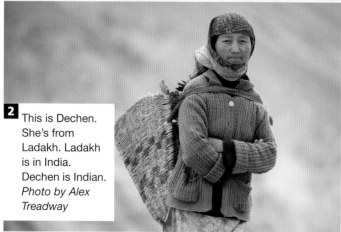

2 This is Dechen. She's from Ladakh. Ladakh is in India. Dechen is Indian.
Photo by Alex Treadway

Vocabulary **countries and nationalities**

3 🔊 **1.10** Write the countries and nationalities in the table. Then listen and check.

British   China   Spanish   the United States

Country	Nationality
Brazil	Brazilian
Canada	Canadian
....	Chinese
Egypt	Egyptian
France	French
Germany	German
Great Britain	
Italy	Italian
Japan	Japanese
Mexico	Mexican
Oman	Omani
Spain	
....	American

4 Pronunciation **word stress**

🔊 **1.11** Listen and repeat the countries from Exercise 3. Notice the stress.

Grammar *he/she/it + is*

▶ *HE/SHE/IT + IS*		
He		from India.
She	**is**	Indian.
It		in India.
(He's, She's = He is, She is)		
For further information and practice, see page 161.		

5 Complete the table for you. Then work in pairs. Tell your partner about yourself. Complete the table for your partner.

	You	**Your partner**
Name		
Country		
Nationality		

6 Work in groups of four. Tell the other pair about your partner.

This is Kira. She's from France. She's French.

7 Look at the photos (a–d). Then read the sentences. Write true (T) or false (F).

1 Haruko is from Japan.
2 John is American.
3 Krishnan is Indian.
4 Marina is from China.

8 Write sentences (true or false) like Exercise 7. Read your sentences to your partner.

Haruko is a writer.

False. She's a filmmaker.

Speaking and writing

9 🔊 **1.12** Work in pairs. Do the quiz. Then listen and check.

Toshiba is French.

False. It's Japanese.

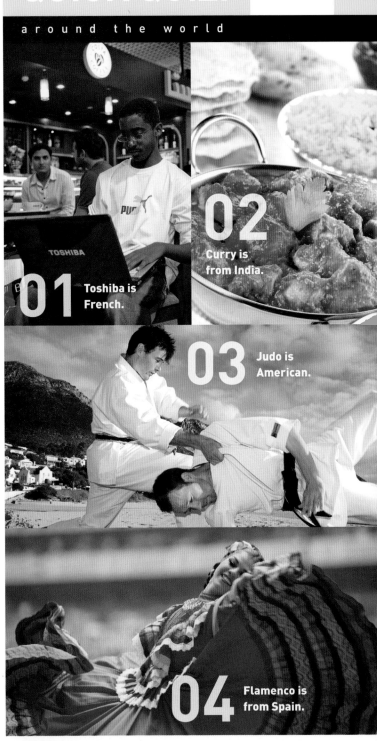

QUICK QUIZ: TRUE OR FALSE

around the world

01 Toshiba is French.

02 Curry is from India.

03 Judo is American.

04 Flamenco is from Spain.

10 Work in pairs. Write an 'Around the world' quiz. Write four sentences. Test the class.

1c International phone calls

Vocabulary continents

1 Look at the map on page 15. Complete the names of the continents.

1 Af........................
2 As........................
3 Au........................
4 E........................
5 N........................ A........................
6 S........................ A........................

2 🔊 **1.13** Listen and repeat the names of the continents.

3 Look at the map again. Complete the sentences.

1 India is in ....
2 Italy is in ....
3 Germany is in ....
4 Canada is in ....
5 Brazil is in ....

4 Work in pairs. Write five sentences (true or false). Test your partner.

Brazil is in Africa.

Reading

5 Read the article on page 15. Underline the names of four countries.

6 Read the article again. Complete the sentences with the correct name.

1 .... is a student.
2 .... is Mexican.
3 .... is an artist.
4 .... is from Brazil.
5 .... is from Canada.
6 .... is a doctor.

7 Word focus *from*

<u>Underline</u> *from* in the sentences. Then match the sentences (1–3) with the pictures (a–c).

1 I'm from Spain.
2 Pizza is from Italy.
3 This phone call is from John.

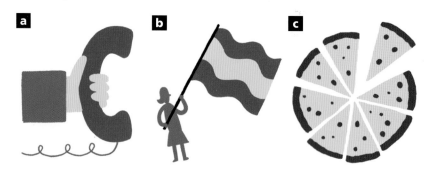

Vocabulary numbers 1–10

8 🔊 **1.14** Write the numbers (1–10). Then listen and repeat the numbers.

0	zero	....	four	....	eight
....	one	....	five	....	nine
....	two	....	six	....	ten
....	three	....	seven		

9 🔊 **1.15** Look at the map and listen to the number. Say the country.

10 🔊 **1.16** Look at the map and listen to the country. Say the number.

Grammar *my, your*

11 🔊 **1.17** Listen to the conversation. Choose the correct mobile phone number (a–c).

a 619 507 713.   b 619 408 713.   c 619 401 623.

12 🔊 **1.17** Listen again. Write the work phone number.

> ▶ **MY, YOUR**
>
> What's **your** phone number?
> **My** mobile number is 619 408 713.
>
> Note: we say *oh* for 0 – not *zero* – in phone numbers.
>
> For further information and practice, see page 161.

Speaking

13 Work in pairs. Ask and answer questions.

mobile number   work number   home number

GEOGRAPHY

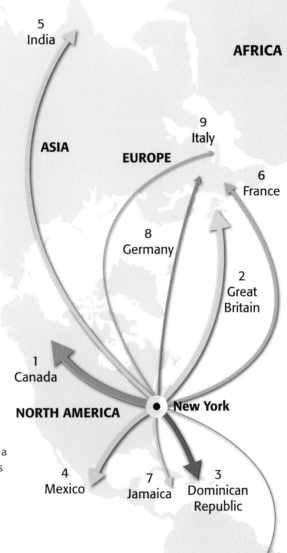

AUSTRALIA

5
India

AFRICA

ASIA

9
Italy

EUROPE

6
France

8
Germany

2
Great
Britain

1
Canada

NORTH AMERICA

New York

4
Mexico

7
Jamaica

3
Dominican
Republic

10
Brazil

SOUTH AMERICA

International phone calls

Anne-Marie Blanc is Canadian. She's a student in New York. She telephones her family in Canada. Canada is the number 1 country for international phone calls from New York.

Juan Garcia is a doctor in New York. He's from Mexico. He telephones his family in Mexico.

Nelson Pires is Brazilian. He's an engineer in New York. He telephones his office in Brazil.

Naomi Smith is from Jamaica. She's an artist in New York. She telephones her family in Jamaica on Sunday.

1d Nice to meet you

Vocabulary greetings

1 🎵 **1.18** Write *Bye* and *Hello* in the correct places. Then listen and repeat.

Good morning.

Good afternoon.

Hi.
1 ....

Good evening.

Good night.

Goodbye.
2 ....

Real life personal information (1)

2 🎵 **1.19** Listen to the conversation. Tick (✓) the greetings in Exercise 1.

3 🎵 **1.19** Listen again. Complete the visitor book.

Date	Name	Company	Signature
17.5.2013	Elias Brich	EB Consulting	*E Brich*
18.5.2013	Suzi Lee	New Start	*Suzi Lee*
18.5.2013	James Watt	New Start	*James Watt*
18.5.2013			

4 Pronunciation questions

a 🎵 **1.20** Listen and repeat three questions from the conversation.

b Work in pairs. Look at the audioscript on page 169. Practise the conversation.

5 Look at the expressions for asking for PERSONAL INFORMATION. Complete the questions with these words.

> first   name   phone

> ▶ **PERSONAL INFORMATION**
>
> What's your .... ?
> What's your .... name?
> What's your surname?
> What's your .... number?
> What's your job?
> I'm Liam. / My name's Liam.

6 Work in pairs. Practise the conversation again. Use information from Exercise 3.

Real life meeting people

7 🎵 **1.21** Listen to the conversation. Put the conversation in order.

   a Hi, Katya. How are you?   *1*
   b Nice to meet you too.
   c Fine, thanks. And you?
   d I'm OK. This is Silvia. She's from Madrid.
   e Nice to meet you, Silvia.

8 Work in groups of three. Practise the conversation from Exercise 7. Use your own names.

> ▶ **MEETING PEOPLE**
>
> Hello. / Hi.
> How are you?
> Fine, thanks. / I'm OK.
> This is X.
> Nice to meet you.
> Nice to meet you too.

9 You are at a meeting. Invent an identity: name, job, company, phone number. Talk to people. Write the names and phone numbers of people with the same job.

> *Good afternoon. I'm Vicente.*

> *Nice to meet you.*

1e My ID

Writing an identity badge

1 Look at the ID badge and find:

1　the name of the company
2　the name of the visitor

2 Writing skill capital letters (1)

a Underline the capital letters on the ID badge.

b Write these words in the table.

Brazil	Nelson Pires
Brazilian	Rio de Janeiro
Portuguese	South America

a city	Washington
a continent	North America
a country	the United States of America
a language	English
a name	Carolyn Anderson
a nationality	American

c Rewrite the sentences with the correct capital letters.

1　riyadh is in saudi arabia.
2　maya angelou is a writer.
3　I'm chinese.
4　He's from tokyo.
5　She's from canada.
6　I speak french.

3 Complete the IDs with the information. Use capital letters.

1 dublin
sean booth

2 american
cathy newman

3 paris bangkok sydney
jan sastre

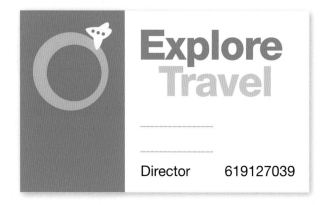

4 Write an ID badge for yourself.

5 Check your badge. Check the capital letters.

1f My top ten photos

Hello. My name's Isha.

Before you watch

1 Work in pairs. Look at this photo. Complete the information about Tom Brooks.

Hi. My name ¹ .... Tom Brooks. I'm ² .... photographer. This ³ .... my top ten – my favourite *National Geographic* photos of people and places.

2 🔊 **1.22** Look at the word box. Listen and repeat the words.

While you watch

3 Watch the video. Tick (✓) the correct column for each photo.

	a man	a woman	people	an animal / animals
Photo 1		✓		
Photo 2				
Photo 3				
Photo 4				
Photo 5				
Photo 6				
Photo 7				
Photo 8				
Photo 9				
Photo 10				

4 Work in pairs. Compare your answers from Exercise 3.

> *Photo 2 is a man.*   *Yes, I agree.*

5 Watch the video again. Choose the correct country.

Photo 1	Nepal / India
Photo 2	China / Mongolia
Photo 3	Mongolia / Nepal
Photo 4	the United States / Canada
Photo 5	Brazil / Bangladesh
Photo 6	Canada / New Zealand
Photo 7	Australia / the United States
Photo 8	South Africa / Namibia
Photo 9	Namibia / Kenya
Photo 10	Kenya / South Africa

6 Work in pairs. Read the sentences. Write true (T) or false (F). Then watch the video again and check.

Photo 1	The photographer is Alex Treadway.
Photo 2	This man is a hunter.
Photo 3	This woman is happy.
Photo 4	This fisherwoman is from Alaska.
Photo 5	This is a photo of water buffalo.
Photo 6	This whale is in the ocean.
Photo 7	This climber is Jimmy Chin.
Photo 8	The photographer is South African.
Photo 9	This photo is in Africa.
Photo 10	Tom says 'This photo is my favourite.'

7 Watch the video again. Choose your favourite photo. Tell your partner.

After you watch

8 Complete the information about three of the photos.

Photo 5 is by Jim Blair. He's ¹ .... American photographer. The photo is in Dhaka in Bangladesh. It's ² .... photo of water buffalo in ³ .... river and ⁴ .... man.

Photo 7 ⁵ .... by Jimmy Chin. This ⁶ .... Kate Rutherford. She's ⁷ .... the United States. She's ⁸ .... climber.

Photo 8 is by David Cartier. ⁹ .... Australian. He's ¹⁰ .... student. This ¹¹ .... a photo of a student too. She's a student ¹² .... South Africa.

9 Write about your favourite photo.

an **animal** (n) /ˈænɪməl/

a **climber** (n) /ˈklaɪmə/

fantastic (adj) /fænˈtastɪk/

a **fisherwoman** (n) /ˈfɪʃəwʊmən/

happy (adj) /ˈhæpi/

a **hunter** (n) /ˈhʌntə/

a **lion** (n) /ˈlaɪən/

a **man** (n) /mæn/

an **ocean** (n) /ˈəʊʃən/

a **river** (n) /ˈrɪvə/

a **water buffalo** (n) /ˈwɔːtə ˌbʌfələʊ/

a **whale** (n) /weɪl/

a **woman** (n) /ˈwʊmən/

UNIT 1 REVIEW

Grammar

1 Complete the sentences with these words.

| I'm | you're | he's | he's | she's | she's | it's | it's |

1 Hi. My name's Rosa. _____ from Brazil.
2 This is Carolyn. _____ an engineer.
3 I'm from Ottowa. _____ in Canada.
4 'My name's Claude Lefevre.'
   'Oh! _____ a writer!'
5 Mattias Lowe is a doctor. _____ from Germany.
6 Marina is from Italy. _____ Italian.
7 This is Nelson. _____ a student.
8 John is from Sydney. _____ in Australia.

2 Circle the correct option.

1 *a / an* book
2 *a / an* country
3 *a / an* explorer
4 *a / an* family
5 *a / an* identity badge
6 *a / an* office
7 *a / an* passport
8 *a / an* phone

I CAN	
introduce people (*be*)	
use *a* and *an* correctly	
use *my* and *your* correctly	

Vocabulary

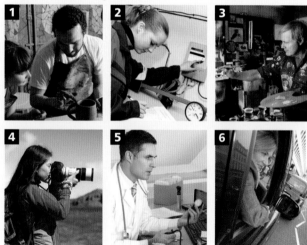

3 Look at the pictures. Complete the sentences with a job, country or nationality.

1 I'm a _____ . I'm from Italy. I'm _____ .
2 Lisa's an _____ . She's French. She's from _____ .
3 Joe's British. He's from _____ . He's an _____ .
4 I'm a _____ . I'm from China. I'm _____ .
5 Enrique is a _____ . He's from Mexico. He's _____ .
6 Sandra's American. She's from _____ . She's a _____ .

4 Work in pairs. Take turns.

Student A: Write five numbers. Then say the numbers to your partner.

Student B: Write the numbers. Then check.

5 Work in pairs. Complete the names of the continents. Spell the names to your partner.

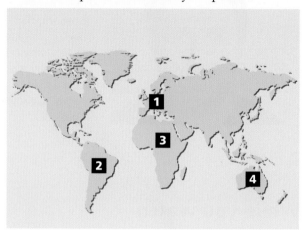

1 _ _ r _ p _
2 S _ _ th _ m _ r _ c _
3 _ fr _ c _
4 _ _ str _ l _ _

I CAN	
talk about jobs, countries and nationalities	
count to ten	
say the alphabet, and spell names and words	

Real life

6 Complete the conversation with a–d.

a Can you spell your surname?
b How are you?
c Nice to meet you too.
d What's your name, please?

A: Hello. I'm from *World Film* magazine.
B: Ah yes! Good <u>morning</u>. [1] _____
A: <u>My name's</u> Amy Lewis.
B: [2] _____
A: Yes. Lewis. L–E–W–I–S.
B: <u>Thanks.</u> Nice to meet you, Amy.
A: [3] _____
B: This is Chanda. She's a photographer.
A: Hi, Chanda. [4] _____
C: <u>Fine, thanks.</u>

I CAN	
ask for and give personal information	
meet and greet people	

Speaking

7 Work in groups of three. Practise the conversation in Exercise 6. Change the <u>underlined</u> words.

Unit 2 Holidays

A beautiful beach on Robinson Crusoe Island in the Pacific Ocean
Photo by Richard Nowitz

FEATURES

1 🔊 **1.23** Look at the photo. Choose the correct option (a–c). Then listen and check.

   a   This is in Canada. It's a beach. It's evening.
   b   This is in France. It's a city. It's night.
   c   This is in Fiji. It's an island. It's morning.

2 🔊 **1.24** Look at these two pictures. Listen and repeat the words.

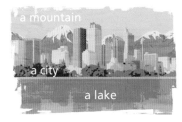

3 Complete the sentences with words from Exercise 2.

   1   Rio de Janeiro is a _____ in Brazil.
   2   Titicaca is a _____ in Bolivia and Peru.
   3   Bondi is a _____ in Australia.
   4   Everest is a _____ in Nepal.

4 Write four sentences about places. Read your sentences to your partner.

   Loch Ness is a lake in Scotland.

2a My holiday

MY HOLIDAY BLOG by Laura

03 JAN

This is in Tunisia. It's beautiful! It's evening. I'm with Brad, Andy and Jessica. We're on a beach. We're happy. Andy and Jessica are Canadian. They're doctors. They're on holiday too.

Reading

1 Work in pairs. Look at the photos. Choose the place (a–c).

a North America
b Europe
c Africa

2 Read about the photo above. Find:

1 the name of the country
2 the names of the people

Grammar *we/they + are*

3 Look at the grammar box. Then look at the blog. Underline the contractions *we're* and *they're*.

▶ *WE/THEY + ARE*		
We	are	in Tunisia.
They		Canadian.
(We're, They're = We are, They are)		
For further information and practice, see page 161.		

4 🔊 **1.25** Complete the sentences. Then listen and check.

1 This is Jane. This is Paul. They _____ Australian.
2 I'm Meera. This is Suri. We _____ from India.
3 In this photo, I'm with my friend Jack. _____ 're in Egypt.
4 Laura is with Brad, Andy and Jessica. _____ on holiday.
5 Jeanne and Claude are from France. _____ French.
6 I'm happy. My friend is happy. _____ happy!

5 Pronunciation *we're, they're*

a 🔊 **1.26** Listen and repeat six sentences.

b Work in pairs. Write three true sentences with *We're*. Read your sentences to a new pair.

We're in Moscow.

6 Read these sentences about the photo on page 22. Write true (T) or false (F). Then correct the false sentences.

1 It isn't Tunisia.
2 They are on a beach.
3 Andy and Jessica aren't from Canada.
4 Laura isn't in the photo.
5 They aren't happy.

Grammar *be* negative forms

7 Look at the grammar box. Then look at the sentences in Exercise 6. What are the negative forms of *is* and *are*?

▶ BE NEGATIVE FORMS		
I	am not ('m not)	
You	are not (aren't)	happy.
He/She/It	is not (isn't)	on a beach.
We/You/They	are not (aren't)	

For further information and practice, see page 162.

8 Complete the blog about the photo below. Use these words.

not   aren't   isn't   isn't

9 Pronunciation *isn't, aren't*

a 🎵 1.27 Listen and repeat the sentences from Exercise 8.

b Write true sentences. Read your sentences to your partner.

We aren't on a beach.

	a student.
	a doctor.
I'm (not)	in a city.
	in a classroom.
You're	in Asia.
You aren't	happy.
We're	on a lake.
We aren't	on a beach.
	on holiday.
	from Morocco.

Speaking

10 Work in groups. Show a photo on your mobile phone to the group. Tell the group about your photo.

This is a photo of my friends, Carlos and Enrique. We're in Egypt.

In this photo, we ¹_____ in Tunisia. We're in Morocco. It ²_____ a beach. It's the Sahara Desert. Andy and Jessica are on a camel trek. Brad ³_____ on the camel trek. He's in a tent. I'm ⁴_____ in this photo.

2b Where are you?

Vocabulary numbers 11–100

1 🔊 **1.28** Write the numbers. Then listen and repeat.

_11_	eleven
_____	twelve
_____	thirteen
_____	fourteen
_____	fifteen
_____	sixteen
_____	seventeen
_____	eighteen
_19_	nineteen

2 🔊 **1.29** Write the numbers in order. Then listen, check and repeat.

eighty	fifty	forty	ninety
seventy	sixty	thirty	twenty

one hundred
_____
_____
_____
_____
_____
_____
_____
_____
ten
zero

3 🔊 **1.30** Look at the temperatures. Then listen. Are the numbers the same – or different?

It's twelve degrees.
the same

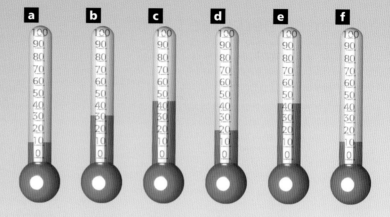

4 🔊 **1.30** Listen again. Write the correct numbers.

5 Work in pairs. Say the correct temperatures to your partner.

6 Complete the sentences with *hot* or *cold*.

1 It's eleven degrees in London today. It's _____ .
2 It's thirty-six degrees in Sydney today. It's _____ .

7 Work in pairs. Make sentences with *hot* and *cold*.

Iceland is cold.

Cairo is hot.

Reading and listening

8 Lorna is Australian. She's on holiday in Europe. Read the conversation. Answer the questions.

1 Where's Lorna?
2 Where's Greg?
3 Where are Kara and Ona?

9 🎵 **1.31** Listen and choose the correct option.

Greg:	Hi! Where are you now? Are you in ¹ *France / Italy*?
Lorna:	Yes, I am. I'm in the Alps. It's beautiful!
Greg:	Are you OK?
Lorna:	No, I'm not. It's ² *two / thirty-two* degrees!
Greg:	Wow! Is it ³ *cold / hot* in your hotel?
Lorna:	No, it isn't. The hotel is nice.
Greg:	It's ⁴ *thirty-six / sixteen* degrees in Sydney today.
Lorna:	Oh! That's ⁵ *hot / cold*!
Greg:	Are Kara and Ona in France?
Lorna:	No, they aren't. They're on a ⁶ *beach / lake* in Morocco!

Grammar *be* questions and short answers

10 Look at the grammar box. Then look at the conversation in Exercise 9. Underline the questions.

▶ **BE QUESTIONS and SHORT ANSWERS**

Am I		Yes, I **am**. No, I**'m not**.
Are you/we/they	in France? cold?	Yes, you/we/they **are**. No, you/we/they **aren't**.
Is she/he/it		Yes, she/he/it **is**. No, she/he/it **isn't**.

For further information and practice, see page 162.

11 Put the words in order to make questions. Then match the questions (1–6) with the answers (a–f).

1 you / OK / are / ?
2 is / in France / Kara / ?
3 in Sydney / you and Paul / are / ?
4 in London / is / Greg / ?
5 Kara and Ona / in Morocco / are / ?
6 nice / your hotel / is / ?

a Yes, they are.
b No, he isn't.
c Yes, I am.
d Yes, it is.
e No, she isn't.
f Yes, we are.

12 Pronunciation *be* questions and short answers

a 🎵 **1.32** Listen and repeat the questions and answers from Exercise 11.

b Work in pairs. Practise the questions and answers.

Speaking

13 Work in pairs. You are on holiday. Have a telephone conversation with your friend.

Student A: Turn to page 153.

Student B: Turn to page 157.

2c A holiday quiz

La Defense, Paris, France

Vocabulary **colours**

1 🔊 **1.33** Match the colours with the numbers. Then listen, check and repeat.

1 **2** **3** **4** **5**

| black | blue | brown | green | grey | orange |
| pink | red | white | yellow | | |

6 **7** **8** **9** **10**

2 Find the colours in the photo.

3 Find six of the colours in the photos on page 27.

Reading

4 Look at the photos on page 27. Find *a car* and *a bus*.

5 Read the quiz on page 27. Match the photos with four sentences.

6 🔊 **1.34** Work in pairs. Complete the sentences in the quiz. Then listen and check.

Grammar **plural nouns**

7 Look at the grammar box. Find these plural nouns in the quiz. Then find four more plural nouns in the quiz.

▶ NOUNS	
Singular	**Plural**
a lake	lakes
a car	cars
a country	countries
a beach	beaches
For further information and practice, see page 162.	

8 Pronunciation **plural nouns**

a 🔊 **1.35** Listen and repeat these nouns.

/s/	/z/	/ɪz/
lakes	cars	beaches
airports	countries	buses

b 🔊 **1.36** Write the plural of these nouns. Then listen and repeat.

a city	a doctor	a friend	a hotel
a mountain	an office	a phone	
a student	a tent		

9 Word focus *in*

Write the expressions in the correct place.

| in Australia | in French | in a hotel |
| in Japanese | in Moscow | in a tent |

1 in English
2 in Europe
3 in a classroom

Speaking

10 Work in pairs. Test your partner. Take turns.

| cities | countries | continents | lakes |
| mountains | | | |

Name three cities.

London, Lima, Bangkok.

A Holiday Quiz

airports   Australia   black   China
Cuba   France   lakes   London

❶ In _____ , cars are old.
❷ In _____ , buses are red.
❸ In Hawaii, beaches are _____ .
❹ In Iceland, the _____ are hot.
❺ Lake Geneva is in two countries – Switzerland and _____ .
❻ The Blue Mountains are in _____ .
❼ Hong Kong, Shanghai and Beijing are cities in _____ .
❽ John Lennon, Charles de Gaulle and John F Kennedy are _____ .

A 1951 Chevy on
Playa Ancon, Cuba

2d Here are your keys

Vocabulary car hire

1 🎵 **1.37** Listen and match 1–5 with a–e.

1 a car registration number
2 an email address
3 an address
4 a postcode
5 keys

3 Park Street
Gateshead
NE2 4AG

To: jamesp@national.org

e PT61 APR

2 Work in pairs.

Student A: Read an email address.

Student B: Identify the email address.

Take turns.

1 smith23@hotmail.com
2 ryan.law@google.co.uk
3 barry@egg.com
4 smnrss@msn.com
5 b.mark@btinternet.com

3 Work in pairs. Ask your partner their address, postcode, email address and car registration number.

Real life personal information (2)

4 🎵 **1.38** Listen to the conversation. Answer the questions.

1 Is the man from Tokyo?
2 Is he on holiday or on business?

5 🎵 **1.38** Listen again. Choose the correct option.

1 Name: *Mr Sato / Mrs Ono*
2 Postcode: *08597 / 170-3293*
3 Email address: *epsato@hotmail.com / ep@hotmail.co.uk*
4 Car registration number: *BD52 ACR / BD61 ATR*

6 Work in pairs. Look at the audioscript on page 169. Practise the conversation.

> ▶ **PERSONAL INFORMATION**
>
> This is my ID.
> Where are you from?
> Is this your (email) address?
> What's the postcode?
> What's your telephone number in the UK?
> Sign here, please.
> Here's your key.
> The car registration number is BD61 ATR.
> Note: in email addresses we say *at* for @ and *dot* for '.'

7 Pronunciation **syllables**

🎵 **1.39** Listen and repeat these words. Count the syllables.

holiday   ho – li – day = 3

| address | car | email | key | number | telephone |

8 Work in pairs. Practise the conversation again with new information.

Good evening.   Hello, I'm Mrs Ono.

TALK ABOUT ▶ HOLIDAY PHOTOS ▶ ON HOLIDAY ▶ GENERAL KNOWLEDGE ▶ **CAR HIRE**
WRITE ▶ A FORM

2e Contact details

Writing a form

1 Match 1 and 2 with the options (a and b).

  a a hotel online booking form
  b an internet profile

Enya Farrell

Call name: enya123

Mobile phone: 0795 157 963
Home phone: 00 44 161 8542
Email address: enya@bt.com
Country: UK
Contacts: 19

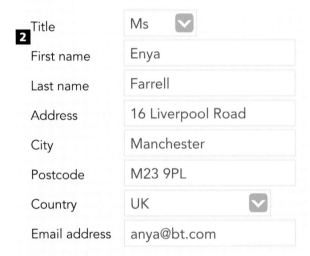

Title	Ms
First name	Enya
Last name	Farrell
Address	16 Liverpool Road
City	Manchester
Postcode	M23 9PL
Country	UK
Email address	anya@bt.com

2 What's your title? Is it Mr, Mrs or Ms?

3 Writing skill capital letters (2)

a Look at the information in form 2. Underline the capital letters.

b Rewrite this information with the correct capital letters.

1 11 hill view   4 judd
2 g12 3xt   5 mr
3 glasgow   6 ryan

4 Complete the college registration form with the information from Exercise 3b.

REGISTRATION FORM

Title _____
First name _____
Last name _____
Address _____
_____
City _____
Postcode _____
Contact number *0733 489 145*
Email address *ryan@judd.co.uk*

5 Complete the online booking form with your own information.

Title	Choose…
First name	
Last name	
Address	
City	
Postcode	
Contact number	
Email address	

6 Check your form. Check the capital letters.

2f Antarctica

People and penguins in Antarctica

Before you watch

1 Look at the photo and the caption on page 30. What are the animals?

2 🔊 **1.40** Look at the word box. Listen and repeat the words.

3 Look at the map. Write the number (1–4) next to the place.

Africa	Australia	New Zealand	South America

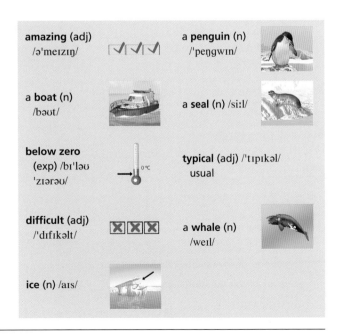

Antarctica
South Pole

While you watch

4 Watch the video without sound. Write at least five words.

white

5 Work in pairs. Read your words to your partner. Watch the video again. Check your partner's words.

6 Watch and listen to the video. Listen to information about these things. Put the words in the order you hear them.

a	animals	d	temperatures	*1*
b	beaches	e	the sea	
c	boats			

7 Read the sentences. Watch the video again. Write true (T) or false (F).

1 The typical temperatures in Antarctica are 90 degrees below zero.
2 The people on the boat are scientists.
3 The animals in the sea are whales and penguins.
4 The temperature of the sea in Antarctica is from two degrees below zero to ten degrees.

8 Read the sentences. Underline the correct option. Watch the video again. Check your answers.
1 Antarctica *is / isn't* a continent.
2 Antarctica *is / isn't* a good place for scientists and explorers.
3 The beaches *are / aren't* yellow.
4 Cold temperatures *are / aren't* good for the animals.

After you watch

9 Work in pairs. Test your memory. Ask and answer the questions.

1 Where are the boats from?
2 What colour are penguins?
3 What colour are whales?
4 What colour is ice?

10 Work in pairs. Write questions about Antarctica with these words.

1 mountains / beautiful
2 the beaches / nice
3 animals / amazing
4 Antarctica / a good place for a holiday

11 Work as a class. Ask three people your questions. Write their names and answers.

> Are the mountains beautiful?

> Yes, they are.   No, they aren't.

---

amazing (adj) /əˈmeɪzɪŋ/ ✓✓✓	a penguin (n) /ˈpeŋgwɪn/
a boat (n) /bəʊt/	a seal (n) /siːl/
below zero (exp) /bɪˈləʊ ˈzɪərəʊ/	typical (adj) /ˈtɪpɪkəl/ usual
difficult (adj) /ˈdɪfɪkəlt/ ✗✗✗	a whale (n) /weɪl/
ice (n) /aɪs/	

Grammar

1 Complete the texts with the words. Then match the photo with Greg or Kara.

> 'm   isn't   not   we're

GREG
I'm in the mountains. I ¹ _____ with my friends. We're in Canada. ² _____ on holiday. I'm ³ _____ happy – the hotel ⁴ _____ nice.

> are   aren't   isn't   they're   we

KARA
I'm in Brazil with my friends Jorge and Ana. ⁵ _____ Brazilian. I'm on holiday. Jorge and Ana ⁶ _____ on holiday. ⁷ _____ 're in Rio de Janeiro. The beaches ⁸ _____ beautiful. The sea ⁹ _____ cold – it's hot!

2 Write questions.

1 you / a student?
2 your teacher / American?
3 we / in an office?
4 you / from Europe?
5 we / in Asia?
6 your friends / teachers?
7 this classroom / cold?
8 you / OK?

3 Work in pairs. Ask and answer the questions in Exercise 2.

4 Write the plurals.

1 airport _____
2 beach _____
3 bus _____
4 car _____
5 city _____
6 country _____
7 friend _____
8 lake _____
9 office _____
10 photo _____

I CAN	
talk about more than one person (we, you, they)	
ask and answer questions (be)	
use regular plural nouns	

Vocabulary

5 Write the numbers.

a eleven + twelve = _____
b twenty-three + sixty = _____
c forty-five + fifteen = _____
d thirty-eight + fifty-one = _____
e seventy + nineteen = _____
f sixteen + thirteen = _____

6 Choose the correct colour.

1 My car is *red / yellow*.
2 My phone is *grey / black*.
3 The mountains are *white / pink*.
4 The buses are *yellow / green*.
5 The lake is *brown / blue*.
6 The boats are *orange / red*.

I CAN	
count from eleven to one hundred	
say the colours of objects	

Real life

7 Complete 1–4 with four of these words. Then match 1–4 with a–d.

> a   are   is   my   postcode   your

1 Where you from?
2 this your address in the UK?
3 What's the?
4 Here are keys.

a NE45 8FP.
b Thank you.
c I'm from Poland.
d Yes, it is.

8 Work in pairs. Practise the exchanges in Exercise 7.

I CAN	
ask for and give personal information	
hire a car	

Speaking

9 Work in pairs.

Student A: You are a car hire receptionist.

Student B: You are a customer.

Ask and answer questions to complete the car hire form. Take turns.

SuperCar

title	
first name	
last name	
address	
city	
postcode	
contact number	
email address	

Unit 3 Families

A family trip in Jamba, India
Photo by Carla Dedominicis

FEATURES

1 🔊 **1.41** Look at the photo and read the information about the family. Complete the information for Ravi and Mohan. Then listen and check.

Danvir and Mohan are brothers. Ravi and Danvir are father and son. Ravi and Mohan are _____ and _____ .

2 🔊 **1.42** Write the words in the correct place. Then listen and repeat.

daughter	parents	sister

♂   ♀

brother   _____
son   _____
father   &   mother   =   _____

3 Complete the sentences with a family word.

1 I'm a _____ .
2 I'm not a _____ .

4 Work in pairs. Read your sentences to your partner.

I'm a father. I'm a brother.   *I'm a sister. I'm not a mother.*

3a Unusual families

Vocabulary **family**

1 Look at the words. Add *grand-* to six of the words to make words for more family members.

brother	child	cousin
daughter	father	mother
parent	sister	son

2 Look at the Cousteau family tree. Find the names of:

1 the grandparents
2 two grandsons
3 two granddaughters
4 two brothers
5 four cousins

The Cousteau family

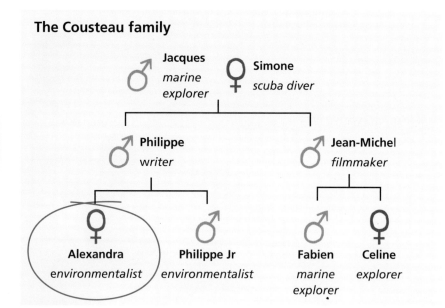

Reading and listening

3 🎧 **1.43** The woman in the photo is Alexandra Cousteau. Look at the family tree. Tick (✓) the correct options (a–d) about Alexandra. Then listen and check.

Who's Alexandra?
a She's Jacques Cousteau's daughter.
b She's Philippe's daughter.
c She's Philippe Jr's sister.
d She's Simone's mother.

4 🎧 **1.43** Listen again. Match A and B to make sentences.

A	B
Alexandra Cousteau is	Philippe's children.
Jean-Michel Cousteau is	Jean-Michel's children.
Fabien and Celine are	Jacques Cousteau's granddaughter.
Alexandra and Philippe Jr. are	Alexandra's brother.
Philippe Jr is	Jacques Cousteau's son.

Grammar **possessive** *'s*

5 Look at the grammar box. Then look at the sentences in Exercise 4. Find *'s* five times.

> ▶ **POSSESSIVE 'S**
>
> Alexandra Cousteau is Jacques Cousteau**'s** granddaughter.
>
> For further information and practice, see page 162.

6 Explain the use of *'s* in these sentences.

1 Who's Celine?
2 She's Fabien's sister.

7 Work in pairs. Test your memory.

> Who's Jacques?

> He's Alexandra's grandfather.

8 Look at the photo. Then look at the example. Write sentences about this family.

Example: Odval – Altan
Odval is Altan's mother.

1 Altan – Batu   3 Kushi – Altan
2 Altan – Odval   4 Odval – Batu

9 Pronunciation possessive *'s*

🔊 **1.44** Listen and repeat the sentences from Exercise 8.

Speaking and writing

10 Work in pairs. Draw your family tree. Tell your partner about people in your family.

> Who's David?

> He's my sister's son.

11 Write about your family tree.

Four generations of a family in Mongolia

Odval

Batu

Kushi

Altan

3b Celebrations

Vocabulary **months and ages**

1 🔊 **1.45** Look at the diary page. Write the months in the correct place. Then listen and check.

August	December	February	June	November

FAMILY EVENTS

January	
	Jim's birthday (49)
March	Rory's birthday (34)
April	Sue and Colin's wedding anniversary
May	Jack and Rosie's wedding anniversary
	Matt's birthday (19)
July	
	Eve's birthday (21!)
September	
October	
	Kate and Paul's wedding anniversary
	our wedding anniversary

2 🔊 **1.46** Listen and repeat the months.

3 Work in pairs. Look at the diary page. Ask and answer questions.

When's Sue and Colin's wedding anniversary?

In April.

4 Write a list of five family members. Then work in pairs. Exchange lists. Take turns to ask and answer questions about people's ages.

mother
grandmother
sister – Pilar
sister – Erika
brother

How old is your sister Erika?

She's twenty-three.

Reading

5 Look at the photo of a wedding. Find:

the bride	the groom	a boy	a girl

6 Read about the wedding. Complete the sentences with five of these words.

bride	cousin	groom	husband
wedding	wife		

1 This is Jao and Sunisa's _____ .
2 The _____ 's name is Sunisa.
3 The _____ 's name is Jao.
4 Deng is Jao's _____ .
5 Deng's _____ is at the wedding.

Celebrations around the world

This is a wedding in Thailand in October 2010. The bride is 23 years old. Her name's Sunisa. The groom is 30 years old. His name's Jao. Their family and friends are at the wedding. Jao's cousin Deng is there with his wife and their children. 'Today we are all happy,' says Deng.

Grammar *his, her, our, their*

7 Look at the sentences in the grammar box. When do we use *his* and *her*? When do we use *our* and *their*?

> ▶ **HIS, HER, OUR, THEIR**
>
> He is the groom. **His** name's Jao.
> She is the bride. **Her** name's Sunisa.
> They are from Thailand. This is a photo of **their** wedding.
> We are married. **Our** wedding anniversary is in June.
>
> For further information and practice, see page 162.

8 Complete the sentences with *his, her, our* and *their*.

1   Deng's daughter is three. _____ name's Areva.
2   Sunisa's father is fifty. _____ name's Thaksin .
3   This is a photo of my father. _____ name's Andrew.
4   Kate and Paul are parents. _____ baby's name is Louisa.
5   My sister and I are twins. _____ birthday is the same day.
6   My sister's name is Ariadna. _____ son's name is Pol.

9 Look at the answers. Complete the questions about the people in the photo with these words.

he	her	his	she	their	they

1   'Where are _____ ?'
    'In Thailand.'
2   'What's _____ name?'
    'Jao.'
3   'What are _____ names?'
    'Sunisa and Areva.'
4   'What's _____ husband's name?'
    'Jao.'
5   'How old is _____ ?'
    'He's 30.'
6   'Who is _____ ?'
    'Deng's daughter.'

Speaking

10 Work in pairs. Ask and answer questions about two weddings.

Student A: Turn to page 153.

Student B: Turn to page 157.

TALK ABOUT ▶ YOUR FAMILY TREE ▶ A WEDDING ▶ YOUR FAMILY PYRAMID ▶ SPECIAL OCCASIONS
WRITE ▶ A GREETINGS CARD

3c Young and old

Vocabulary **adjectives**

1 🎵 **1.47** Match these adjectives with the pictures (1–6). Then listen, check and repeat.

| big | old | poor | rich | small | young |

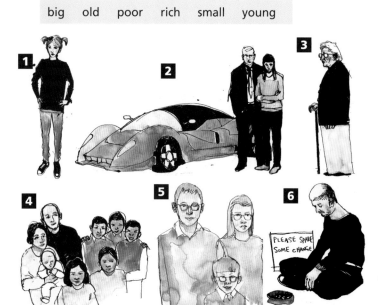

2 Find three pairs of opposite adjectives in Exercise 1.

3 Write three sentences with words from Exercise 1. Then read your sentences to your partner.

> *My grandfather isn't young.*

Reading

4 Read the article on page 39. <u>Underline</u> the names of two countries.

5 What is the information in the diagrams? Choose the correct option (a or b).

a The ages of people in two different countries.
b The family size in two different countries.

6 Read the article again. Answer the questions.

1 Where are families big?
2 Where are people old?

7 Work in groups. Answer the questions.

1 Are families in your country big or small?
2 Are people old or young?

> *I'm from Italy. In my country, families are small.*

Grammar **irregular plural nouns**

8 Look at the grammar box. <u>Underline</u> examples of these nouns in the article on page 39.

> ▶ **IRREGULAR PLURAL NOUNS**
>
> a child → two **children**
> a man → three **men**
> a woman → four **women**
> a person → five **people**
>
> For further information and practice, see page 163.

9 Choose the correct option.

1 Daughters and mothers are *men* / *women*.
2 Grandsons and grandfathers are *men* / *women*.
3 Boys and girls are *children* / *men*.

10 Word focus *at*

🎵 **1.48** Look at the expressions with *at*. Complete the exchanges with three of the expressions. Then listen and check.

| at a meeting | at home |
| at a wedding | at work |

1 A: Where are Paul and Jen today?
  B: They're _____ _____
     _____ . The bride is Jen's sister.

2 A: Is Jack in the office this week?
  B: No, he's _____ _____
     _____ in Paris.

3 A: Where are you?
  B: We're _____ _____ ! My
     parents are here.

11 Pronunciation **linking with** *at*

🎵 **1.49** Listen and repeat these sentences.

1 They're at_a wedding.
2 He's at_a meeting.

Speaking

12 Work in pairs. Draw an age pyramid for your family. Tell your partner about it.

> *The people in my family are all young. I'm twenty-one.*

FAMILIES AROUND THE WORLD ARE DIFFERENT

This is Mulogo and his friends. They are from Uganda. Their families are big – with seven or eight children. Mulogo's brothers and sisters are under sixteen years old. In Uganda, people are young. Half the people are under fifteen. Uganda is a poor country.

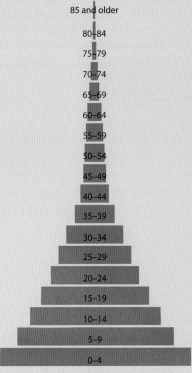

| 85 and older |
| 80–84 |
| 75–79 |
| 70–74 |
| 65–69 |
| 60–64 |
| 55–59 |
| 50–54 |
| 45–49 |
| 40–44 |
| 35–39 |
| 30–34 |
| 25–29 |
| 20–24 |
| 15–19 |
| 10–14 |
| 5–9 |
| 0–4 |

UGANDA

JAPAN

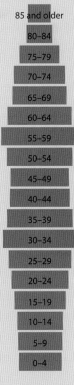

| 85 and older |
| 80–84 |
| 75–79 |
| 70–74 |
| 65–69 |
| 60–64 |
| 55–59 |
| 50–54 |
| 45–49 |
| 40–44 |
| 35–39 |
| 30–34 |
| 25–29 |
| 20–24 |
| 15–19 |
| 10–14 |
| 5–9 |
| 0–4 |

This is Amaya. She's Japanese. Her family is small – one daughter, one son and one grandson. Japan is a rich country. In Japan, people are old. Twenty per cent of the people are over sixty-five. In rich countries, people are old.

TALK ABOUT ▶ YOUR FAMILY TREE ▶ A WEDDING ▶ YOUR FAMILY PYRAMID ▶ SPECIAL OCCASIONS

WRITE ▶ A GREETINGS CARD

3d Congratulations!

Vocabulary **special occasions**

1 🔊 **1.50** Look at these words. Then look at the photo and listen to a conversation. What's the special occasion?

> a new baby
> a birthday
> a party
> a wedding
> a wedding anniversary
> an engagement

2 🔊 **1.50** Put the conversation in order. Then listen again and check.

- a Ah, she's lovely. What's her name?
- b Congratulations!
- c Hello, Juba.
- d It's Juba.
- e Thank you. We're very happy.

Real life **special occasions**

3 🔊 **1.51** Listen to three more conversations. Number (1–3) the occasions in Exercise 1.

4 🔊 **1.51** Look at the expressions for SPECIAL OCCASIONS. Listen again. Write the number of the conversation.

> ▶ **SPECIAL OCCASIONS**
>
> Congratulations!
> Happy Birthday!
> Happy Anniversary!
> I'm very happy for you.
> How old are you?
> When's the wedding?

5 Pronunciation exclamations

a 🔊 **1.52** Listen and repeat three expressions for SPECIAL OCCASIONS.

b Work in pairs. Look at the audioscripts on page 170. Practise the conversations.

Real life **giving and accepting presents**

6 Work in pairs. Answer the questions.

1 Is it traditional to give presents in your country?
2 What are special occasions for giving presents?
3 What's a good present for these special occasions?

> a new baby
> new parents
> your best friend's birthday
> your cousin's wedding
> your parents' wedding anniversary

7 🔊 **1.53** Look at the occasions in Exercise 1 again. Listen to the conversation. What is the occasion?

8 🔊 **1.53** Listen again. Tick (✓) the expressions for GIVING AND ACCEPTING PRESENTS.

> ▶ **GIVING AND ACCEPTING PRESENTS**
>
> **This is for** you / the baby.
> **That's** lovely / very kind.
> You're welcome. / It's a pleasure.
> Thanks. / Thank you very much.

9 Work in pairs. Choose a special occasion. Practise the conversation from Exercise 7. Take turns.

> *Hi. This is for …*

TALK ABOUT ▶ YOUR FAMILY TREE ▶ A WEDDING ▶ YOUR FAMILY PYRAMID ▶ SPECIAL OCCASIONS
WRITE ▶ A GREETINGS CARD

3e Best wishes

Writing a greetings card

1 Writing skill contractions

a <u>Underline</u> the contractions in these sentences. What's the missing letter?

1 I'm Australian.
2 She's French.
3 It isn't my birthday.
4 What's your name?
5 They're engaged.
6 Who's this?
7 You aren't married.
8 Where's your husband?

b Find and <u>underline</u> seven contractions in these messages.

1

It's Harry's birthday tomorrow. He's with his grandparents in London. What's their address?

2

Diana and Albert are engaged. They're really happy! The engagement party's at Albert's house.

3

Ingrid and Karl's wedding's in June. Sonia's the bridesmaid. I'm the best man!

c Rewrite these messages. Use contractions.

1

It is Karin's birthday tomorrow. She is twenty-one. Where is her present?

2

I am engaged to Peter. Our wedding is in May.

3

Hi. What is Katya's husband's name? Is it Bruno or Silvio? Thanks.

2 Read the greeting. Answer the questions.

1 What's the occasion?
2 Who's the card from?
3 Who's the card to?

To Harry

Many happy returns on your birthday!

Love and best wishes from Katya and Bruno

3 Write a card for Diana and Albert, and for Karin. Use these words. You can use some words more than once.

best wishes   birthday   congratulations
engagement   from   love
many happy returns   on   to   your

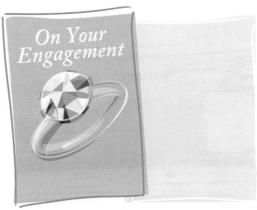

4 Read your cards. Check the capital letters.

5 Work in pairs. Compare your cards with your partner's cards.

A Mongolian family

3f

Mongolian children in Ulaanbaatar

Before you watch

1 Read about Mongolia. Complete the article with three of these words.

> country   family   hot   people

Mongolia

Mongolia is a ¹ _____ in Asia. It's big. It's cold in January and it's ² _____ in July. The capital of Mongolia is Ulaanbaatar. Sixty per cent of the ³ _____ are under thirty. Forty per cent of the people are in Ulaanbaatar.

2 💿 **1.54** Look at the word box. Listen and repeat the words.

3 Look at the photo on page 42. Find:

> a ger   children   houses

While you watch

4 Watch the video. Tick (✓) the things you see.

> a ger   a city
> children   a wedding
> animals   mountains

5 The young man's name is Ochkhuu Genen. Watch the video again. Match the names with the people.

1	Anuka	his wife's mother
2	Norvoo	his daughter
3	Jaya	his wife's father
4	Chantsal	his wife

6 Read the questions. Watch the video again. Choose the correct option (a–c).

1 Where is Ochkhuu's ger?
   a in Ulaanbaatar   c in the mountains
   b in the country

2 How old is Ochkhuu's daughter?
   a two years old   c ten years old
   b six years old

3 How old are Norvoo's parents?
   a fifty-five years old c sixty-five years old
   b sixty years old

4 What is Norvoo's father's job?
   a a taxi driver   c a teacher
   b a farmer

5 What is Ochkhuu's job?
   a a taxi driver   c a teacher
   b a farmer

After you watch

7 Work in pairs. Answer the questions.

1 Is Ochkhuu's family big or small?
2 Are Ochkhuu's parents young or old?

8 Work in pairs.

Student A: Look at photo A. You are in Mongolia. These people are your neighbours. What are their names and ages? What are the relationships?

Tell your partner about the people in the photo.

Student B: Look at photo B. You are in the United States. These people are your neighbours. What are their names and ages? What are the relationships?

Tell your partner about the people in the photo.

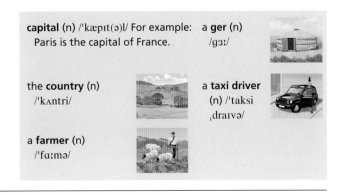

capital (n) /ˈkæpɪt(ə)l/ For example: Paris is the capital of France.

a ger (n) /ɡɜː/

the country (n) /ˈkʌntri/

a taxi driver (n) /ˈtaksi ˌdraɪvə/

a farmer (n) /ˈfɑːmə/

UNIT 3 REVIEW

Grammar

1 Complete the sentences.

1 Look at the photo. This is _____ .
   (Jin / family)

2 This is _____ .
   (Sandra / car)

3 They're _____ .
   (Toni / keys)

4 Is this _____ ?
   (Diana / phone)

5 This is _____ .
   (Michael / passport)

6 Is this _____ ?
   (Enya / email address)   enya@bt.com

2 Complete the sentences with these words.

he's	her	his	our	their	they're

1 This card is for Ellie and Greg. What's _____ address?
2 Suzi and Ryan are engaged. _____ very happy!
3 It's David's birthday. The party's at _____ house.
4 Dirk and I are married. It's _____ anniversary in March.
5 It's my grandfather's birthday today. _____ eighty-nine.
6 'Your baby is lovely! What's _____ name?' 'It's Ana.'

I CAN	
talk about families and possessions (possessive 's and possessive adjectives)	
use irregular plural nouns	

Vocabulary

3 Match the words for women with the words for men.

♀   ♂

bride	brother
daughter	father
grandmother	grandfather
mother	groom
sister	husband
wife	son

4 Work in pairs. Take turns.

Student A: Say a month.

Student B: Say the next month.

5 Choose the correct option.

1 Our class is *big / small* – 38 students!
2 'Are your grandparents *old / young*?' 'Yes, they are. They're 89 and 92.'
3 We aren't rich. We're *big / poor*.
4 My children are *small / young* – five and six years old.
5 This wedding is *rich / small* – the bride and groom and their families.

I CAN	
talk about my family	
talk about months and ages	
describe people	

Real life

6 Put the words in order. Then match 1–4 with a–d.

1 the / is / wedding / when / ?
2 are / how old / you / ?
3 for / this / is / you / .
4 is / pleasure / it / a / .

a are / welcome / you / .
b am / eighteen / I / .
c in / is / July / it / .
d very / kind / is / that / .

7 Work in pairs. Practise the exchanges in Exercise 6. Use contractions.

I CAN	
talk about special occasions	
give and accept presents	

Speaking

8 Write the names of people from three generations in your family. Then work in pairs. Ask and answer questions about the names. Use *who* and *how old*.

The Pearl TV tower and the Huang Pu river in Shanghai, China
Photo by Justin Guariglia

FEATURES

1 Look at the photo. Find these things:

> buildings   a river   a tower

2 Read the photo caption. Find the name of the city and the country.

3 🔊 1.55 Read the sentences. Then listen. Are the sentences true (T) or false (F)?

1 Shanghai is the capital of China.
2 Shanghai isn't rich.
3 The buildings in Shanghai are old.
4 The Pearl TV tower is famous.

4 Work in pairs. Tell your partner about famous things in your town.

> *I'm from Paris. The Eiffel Tower is famous.*

4a In the city

Vocabulary places in a town

1 🔊 **1.56** Look at the words and pictures. Listen and number the words.

a bank	a bus station
a café	a car park
a cinema	a market
a museum	a park
an information centre	a train station

2 🔊 **1.56** Listen again and repeat the places.

3 Are the places in Exercise 1 in your town? What are their names?

The British Museum.

Reading

4 Look at the information about Penbridge town centre and read the comments. Complete the sentences with the places in the comments.

1 The .... is great.
2 The .... is new.
3 The .... is old.
4 The .... is in Oxford Street.

a bank

b Transport Museum

c bus station

d Royal Café

e car park

f City Information Centre

g Roxy Cinema

h Central Market

i train station

j Green Park

The museum isn't very good. It's old. It's near the train station. *Berta*

This café is great! It's next to a cinema. *Artem*

Grammar prepositions of place

5 Look at the grammar box. Then look at the comments about Penbridge. <u>Underline</u> the prepositions.

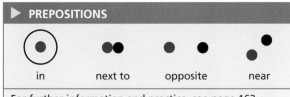

▶ **PREPOSITIONS**

| in | next to | opposite | near |

For further information and practice, see page 163.

6 Look at the map. Are the sentences true (T) or false (F)?

1 The café is next to the cinema.
2 The museum is in London Street.
3 The park is near the information centre.
4 The market is opposite the cinema.

7 Look at the map. Choose the correct option.

1 The bank is *next to / opposite* the market.
2 The cinema is *in / near* London Street.
3 The car park is *near / next to* the museum.
4 The information centre is *next to / opposite* the bus station.
5 The bus station is *in / next to* the park.
6 The train station is *opposite / near* the museum.

8 🔊 **1.57** Listen to four conversations about these places. Write the number of the conversation (1–4) next to the places.

a bank
b car park
c information centre
d train station

9 🔊 **1.57** Listen again. Look at the map. Is the information correct?

Speaking

10 Work in pairs. Look at the audioscript on page 170. Practise the conversations from Exercise 8.

11 Work in pairs. Ask and answer questions about places on the map.

Excuse me?

> *Yes?*

Where's the market?

12 Work in pairs. Ask and answer questions about four places in your town.

Where's the Coffee Pot café?

> *I'm not sure!*

PENBRIDGE TOWN CENTRE

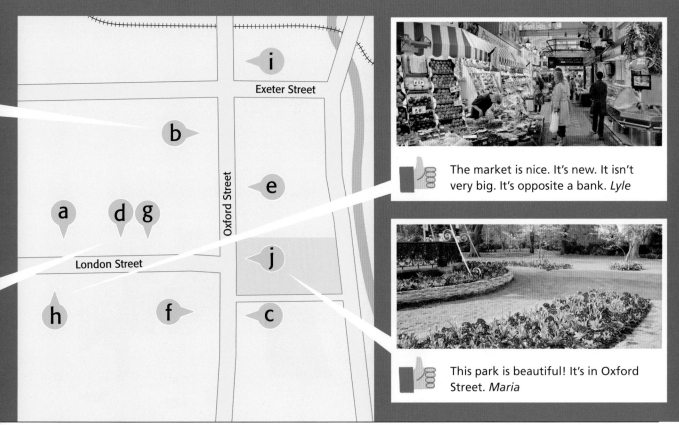

Exeter Street

Oxford Street

London Street

The market is nice. It's new. It isn't very big. It's opposite a bank. *Lyle*

This park is beautiful! It's in Oxford Street. *Maria*

4b Tourist information

Listening

1 🎵 **1.58** Listen to a conversation in a Tourist Information Centre. Put the conversation in order.

a Good morning.
b Is **this** a map of the city?
c Hi.   *1*
d No, it isn't. **That's** a map of the city.
e OK. And where's Big Ben?
f No, it isn't. It isn't open to tourists.
g Oh yes. Is it open on Sunday?
h It's near the River Thames … here it is.

Grammar *this, that*

> ▶ **THIS, THAT**
>
> Is **this** a map of the city?
>
> **That's** a map of the city.
>
> For further information and practice, see page 163.

2 🎵 **1.59** Complete the conversations with *this* and *that*. Then listen and check.

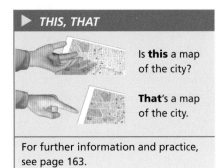

Excuse me. Is _____ a map of London?

1 Yes, it is.

3 Pronunciation *th* /ð/

a 🎵 **1.59** Listen and repeat the conversations from Exercise 2.

b Practise the *th* sound in these words.

> this   that   there   they

Vocabulary **days of the week**

4 🎵 **1.60** Put the days of the week in order. Then listen, check and repeat.

Example: *1 Monday*

> Friday   Monday   Saturday   Sunday   Thursday
> Tuesday   Wednesday

5 🎵 **1.61** Read the questions about places in London. Then listen to the conversation at the Tourist Information Centre. Answer *yes* or *no*.

1 Are museums open on Monday?   yes   no
2 Are shops open every day?   yes   no
3 Are banks open on Sunday?   yes   no

6 Work in pairs. When are places open – and not open – in your country?

> *Banks aren't open on Saturday or Sunday.*

Is _____ a train timetable?

Is _____ guidebook in English?

Where?

2 No, it's a bus timetable.

The book next to you.

No, it isn't. It's in Spanish.

3

The Tower of Pisa

Big Ben

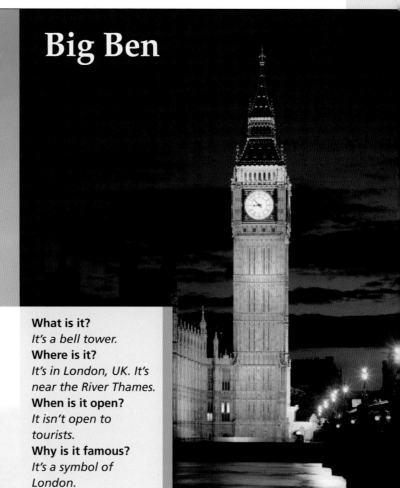

What is it?
It's a bell tower.
Where is it?
It's in Pisa, Italy.
It's next to the cathedral.
When is it open?
It's open every day.
Why is it famous?
It isn't vertical.

What is it?
It's a bell tower.
Where is it?
It's in London, UK. It's near the River Thames.
When is it open?
It isn't open to tourists.
Why is it famous?
It's a symbol of London.

bell (n) /bel/   vertical (n) /ˈvɜːtɪkəl/

Reading

7 Read about two famous towers. Choose the correct option.

1 *Big Ben / The Tower of Pisa* is in a capital city.
2 *Big Ben / The Tower of Pisa* is open to tourists.
3 *Big Ben / The Tower of Pisa* is near a river.

Grammar **question words**

8 Look at the grammar box and the words in **bold** in the questions. Then look at the article about towers. Find the words in **bold** in the article.

▶ QUESTION WORDS
What is it?
Where is it?
When is it open?
Why is it famous?
For further information and practice, see page 163.

9 Complete the questions with the correct question word.

1 Q: _____ are you?
   A: I'm in the park.
2 Q: _____ is the museum open?
   A: Every day.
3 Q: _____ is the name of this street?
   A: Oxford Street.
4 Q: _____ is this place famous?
   A: It's very old.
5 Q: _____ is this?
   A: It's in Italy.
6 Q: _____ is your holiday?
   A: In June.

10 Work in pairs. Ask and answer questions about two more towers.

Student A: Turn to page 154.

Student B: Turn to page 158.

Speaking

11 Work in pairs. Ask and answer questions about famous places you know.

The Giz Galasy tower is in Baku, in Azerbaijan. It's in the Old City.

4c Time zones

Vocabulary the time

1 🔊 **1.62** Match the times with the clocks. Then listen, check and repeat.

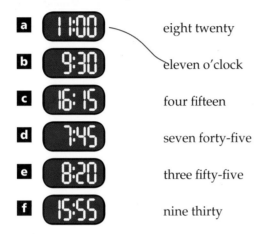

a **11:00** ——— eight twenty

b **9:30** ——— eleven o'clock

c **16:15** ——— four fifteen

d **7:45** ——— seven forty-five

e **8:20** ——— three fifty-five

f **15:55** ——— nine thirty

2 Are the times in Exercise 1 in the morning or afternoon?

3 🔊 **1.63** Listen and write the times.

1 _____   4 _____
2 _____   5 _____
3 _____   6 _____

4 Match the word with the time.

1 midday   00.00
2 midnight   12.00

5 Work in pairs. Ask and answer questions.

| What time is | your the | English class? office open? school open? bus in the morning? train to work? café open? |

Grand Central Station, New York

Information

Reading

6 Read the article and look at the map on page 51. Where is the International Date Line?

7 Read the article again. Look at the time in London. Then write the names of the two cities.

London: 12.00

1 _____ : 20.00   2 _____ : 04.00

8 Work in pairs. It's midday in London. What time is it in these places?

> Cairo   Sydney   Rio de Janeiro   Japan
> Argentina   South Africa

In Cairo, it's two o'clock in the afternoon.

9 What time and day is it where you are now? What time and day is it in London now?

10 Word focus *of*

a Underline *of* in the sentences. Then match the sentences (1–4) with the pictures (a–d).

1 What's the name *of* this street?
2 Rome is the capital *of* Italy.
3 It's a symbol *of* London.
4 This is a map *of* the city.

a PARIS   b   c OXFORD STREET W1 · CITY OF WESTMINSTER ·   d

b Complete the sentences. Then tell your partner.

1 The name of my street is _____ .
2 The capital of my country is _____ .
3 _____ is a symbol of my _____ .

Speaking

11 Work in pairs. Talk about your city at different times of the day.

Student A: Say a time.

Student B: Make sentences.

Take turns.

> *Five o'clock in the afternoon.*

> *Shops are open. Children aren't at school.*

TIME ZONES

In London, it's twelve o'clock midday. Shops and offices are open. People are at work. Children are at school. In Hong Kong, it's eight o'clock in the evening. Schools are closed and children are at home. People are in cafés and restaurants. In Los Angeles, it's four o'clock in the morning. People aren't at work. They're at home.

The time is different in the 24 time zones around the world. The International Date Line is from north to south 'in' the Pacific Ocean. The Date Line is the end of one day and the beginning of the next day. It's 80 kilometres from Russia to Alaska, but Sunday in Russia is Saturday in Alaska.

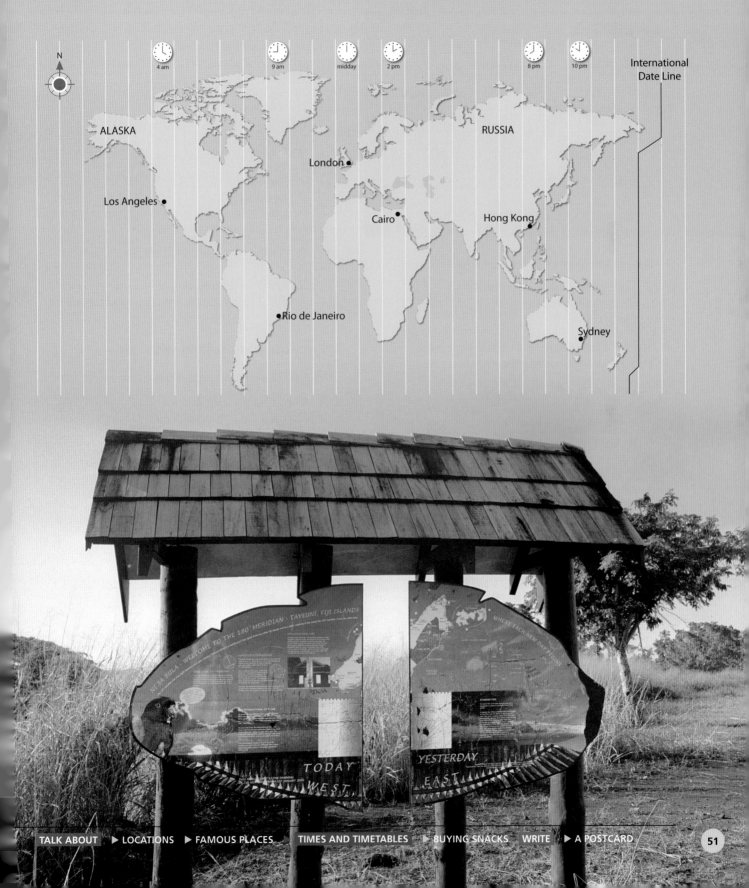

4d Two teas, please

Vocabulary **snacks**

1 Look at the photo. Choose the correct caption (a–c).

a   Fruit juice, India
b   Mint tea, Morocco
c   Black coffee, Turkey

2 🔊 **1.64** Write the words with the pictures (1–7). Then listen, check and repeat.

cake   coffee   fruit juice   mineral water
salad   sandwich   tea

Real life **buying snacks**

3 💿 **1.65** Listen to three conversations. Number the snacks (1–3) in Exercise 2.

4 💿 **1.65** Complete the conversations with expressions for BUYING SNACKS. Then listen again and check.

1   A: Hi. Can I help you?
    B: ¹ _____
    A: ² _____
    B: Small.
    A: Anything else?
    B ³ _____

2   A: Hi. Can I help you?
    B: ⁴ _____
    A: Anything else?
    B: Yes. A salad.
    A: OK. ⁵ _____

3   A: ⁶ _____
    B: A tea and a fruit juice, please.
    A: ⁷ _____
    B: Yes. Two cakes, please.
    A: OK. Here you are. Seven pounds, please.
    B ⁸ _____

5 Pronunciation **linking with** *can*

💿 **1.66** Listen and repeat these sentences.

1   Can‿I help you?
2   Can‿I have a mineral water, please?

> ▶ **BUYING SNACKS**
>
> Can I help you?
> Two coffees, please.
> Can I have a mineral water, please?
> Large or small?
> Anything else?
> No, thanks.
> Four pounds, please.
> Here you are.

6 Work in pairs. Practise the conversations in Exercise 5.

7 Work in pairs. Take turns to buy a snack from your partner.

Hi. Can I help you?

Two teas, please.

4e See you soon

Writing a postcard

1 Read the postcard. Answer the questions.

   1 Who is the postcard to?
   2 Who is it from?
   3 Where are they?

2 Read the postcard again. <u>Underline</u>:

   1 one adjective to describe Thailand
   2 two adjectives to describe the hotel
   3 one adjective to describe the markets
   4 two adjectives to describe people
   5 one adjective to describe the food

3 Writing skill *and*

a Read the postcard again. Circle *and* in two
   sentences.

b Look at the example. Then rewrite the sentences
   with *and*.

   Example: The hotel is small. The hotel is new.
   *The hotel is small **and** new.*

   1 The museums are big. The museums are old.
   2 The park is open on Saturday. The park is open
      on Sunday.
   3 The town is old. The town is beautiful.
   4 It's famous in America. It's famous in Europe.
   5 It's a drink with sugar. It's a drink with mint.

Hi Sandra
We're in Thailand. We're in
Bangkok. It's great! Our hotel
is big and new. It's near the
market on this postcard. The
markets are famous here. Thai
people are nice and friendly.
Oh, and the food is great too.
See you soon.
Jen and Chris

4 Choose a place you know. Write a postcard to your
   partner. Write about three of these things. Use ***and***.

   • the town/city
   • places in the town/city
   • the food
   • the hotel
   • the people

5 Check your postcard. Check the adjectives and the
   spelling.

6 Work in pairs. Exchange postcards. Where is your
   partner?

4f Where's that?

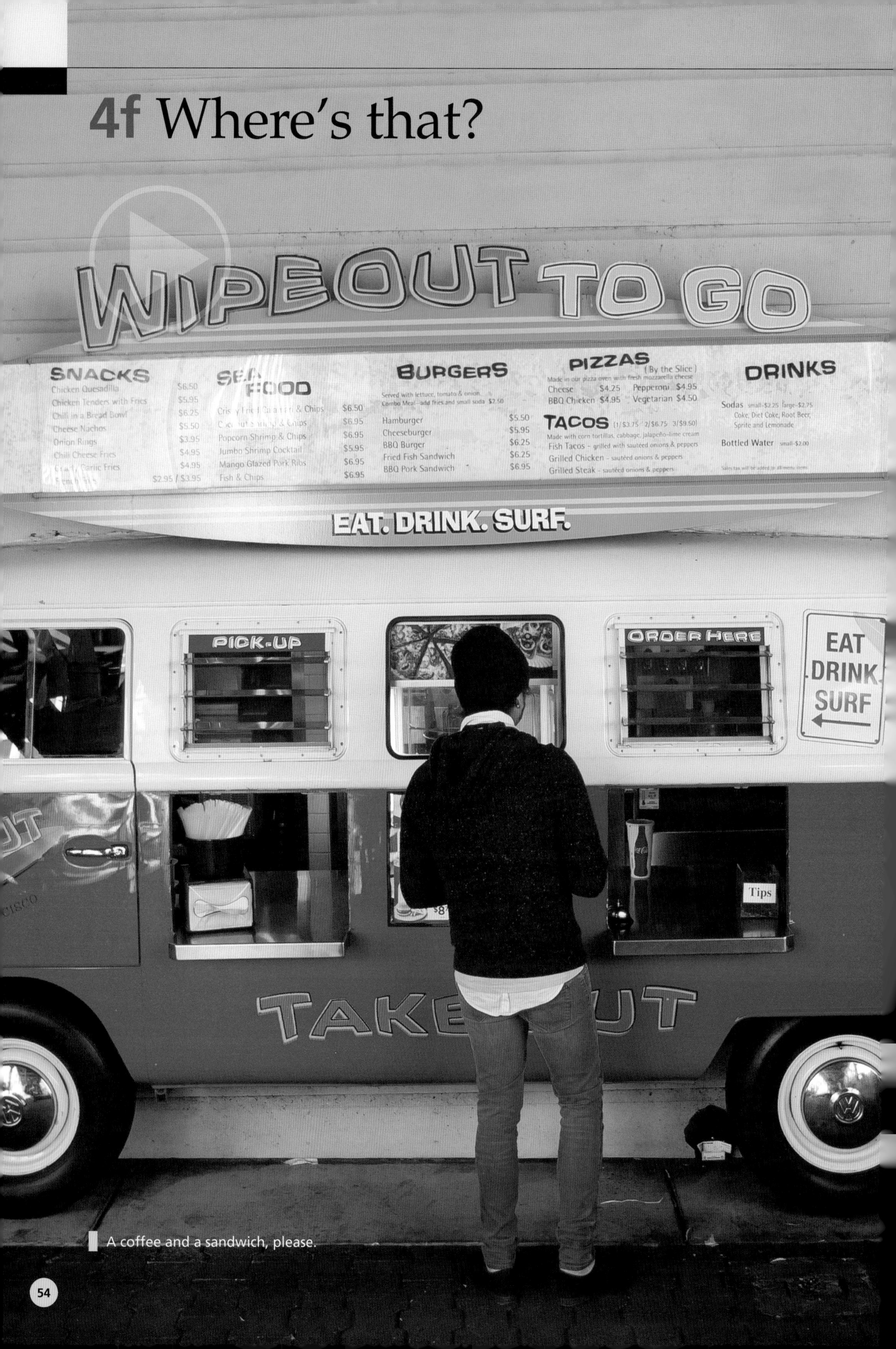

A coffee and a sandwich, please.

Before you watch

1 Look at the photo and the caption on page 54. Find the name for this place in the word box.

2 🔊 **1.67** Look at the word box. Listen and repeat the words.

3 Work in pairs. Are these places in your town? Where?

> a bridge   a shopping street
> a garden   a snack bar

4 Work in pairs. Tick (✓) the things in your city or town.

> a bank
> a bus station
> a café
> a car park
> a cinema
> a market
> a museum
> a park
> an information centre
> a train station

5 This video is a quiz about cities. How many cities?

> ▥ **Where's that?**
>
> ▥ **Four cities around the world.**
>
> ▥ **What are their names?**

While you watch

6 Watch the video. Are the things in your list from Exercise 4 in the video?

7 Watch the video again. Where are the cities? Write the number of the city (1–4) with the continent. Two cities are in one continent.

> America   Asia   Europe

8 Work in pairs. What are the names of the four cities? Choose the correct option (a–c). Do you agree?

> 1   a   Beijing   b   Hong Kong   c   Tokyo
> 2   a   Madrid   b   Paris   c   Rome
> 3   a   New York   b   San Francisco
>   c   Washington
> 4   a   Lisbon   b   London   c   St Petersburg

9 Watch the video again and check.

After you watch

10 Look at the questions and answers from the video. Complete the questions.

> A: That's beautiful. ¹_____'s that?
> B: It's in the city. It's a park with a lake.
>
> A: ²_____'s that? Is that you next to the lake?
> B: No, it isn't.
>
> A: ³_____'s that? A park?
> B: It's a garden – and a nice café next to the garden.
>
> A: Look at the two people. ⁴_____ are they there?
> B: I don't know.
>
> A: ⁵_____ are the people?
> B: They're tourists, I think.

11 Match two places with each city from the video. Then write sentences about one of the cities.

> Atocha Station
> Fisherman's Wharf
> Greenwich Naval College
> Shinjuku district
> the Golden Gate bridge
> the Imperial Palace
> the London Eye and the Houses of Parliament
> the Prado museum

12 Write a postcard from one of the cities in the video.

13 Send your postcard to a classmate.

a **bridge** (n) /brɪdʒ/

a **garden** (n) /'gɑːdən/

lights (n) /laɪts/

a **shopping street** (n) /'ʃɒpɪŋ ˌstriːt/

a **sign** (n) /saɪn/

a **snack bar** (n) /'snæk ˌbɑː/

surf (v) /sɜːf/

UNIT 4 REVIEW

Grammar

1 Read about the café. Then complete the questions.

New!

The Art Café

We are in the Modern Art Museum.
We are next to the Museum Shop.

We are open Monday – Saturday,
10.00 – 18.00. On Sunday we are open
10.00 – 14.30.

Hot and cold snacks.

1 _____ is the café's name?
2 _____ is the café?
3 _____ is in the museum?
4 _____ is the café open?
5 _____ old is the café?

2 Work in pairs. Ask and answer the questions from Exercise 1. Take turns.

3 Look at the pictures. Choose the correct option.

1 Is this / that *the bus to Oxford?*

2 Is this / that *fruit juice?*

3 Is this / that *the train station?*

I don't know!

I CAN	
describe the location of places (prepositions of place)	
use *this* and *that* correctly	
ask and answer questions (question words)	

Vocabulary

4 Complete the words for places in a town.

1 tr _ _ n st _ t _ _ n
2 c _ r p _ rk
3 _ nf _ rm _ t _ _ n c _ ntr _
4 m _ s _ _ m
5 c _ n _ m _
6 m _ rk _ t

5 Work in pairs. Where are the places in Exercise 4 in your town?

6 Work in pairs. Say the days in order. Take turns. Start with Monday.

7 Work in pairs. Take turns.

Student A: Choose a clock and say the time.

Student B: Point to the clock.

08:15   15:45   10:30   12:00

14:20   05:30   22:50   00:00

8 Complete the menu with these snacks.

salad	fruit juice	coffee	sandwiches

The Art Café

Cold drinks
mineral water €1.00
2 _____ €1.50

Snacks
3 _____ €2.00
4 _____ €2.00
cake €1.50

Hot drinks
tea €1.00
1 _____ €1.50

I CAN	
talk about places in a town	
say the days of the week	
say the time	
talk about snacks	

Real life

9 Complete the conversation in a café with a–e.

a Anything else?
b OK. Eight euros, please.
c Large or small?
d Thanks.
e Hello. Can I help you?

A: 1 _____
B: Can I have two teas, please?
A: 2 _____
B: Small, please.
A: 3 _____
B: Yes. Two sandwiches.
A: 4 _____
B: Here you are.
A: 5 _____

I CAN	
buy snacks	

Speaking

10 Work in pairs. Practise the conversation in Exercise 9. Change the snacks.

Unit 5 Inventions

The 'jetman' in the air
Photo by Laurent Gillieron

FEATURES

1 Work in pairs. Look at the photo. What is it?

a   a toy
b   a person
c   a robot

2 🔊 **1.68** Listen to the information about the photo. Check your answer from Exercise 1.

3 🔊 **1.68** Listen again. Choose the correct option.

1   Yves Rossy is from *France / Switzerland*.
2   In the photo, he's above the Swiss *Alps / capital*.
3   He's in the air for *five / nine* minutes.

4 Work in groups. Yves Rossy is an inventor. Name some inventors and their inventions.

Steve Jobs – iPod

5a Robots and people

ROBOTS AND PEOPLE

This is 69-year-old Nabeshima Akiko. She's in a supermarket in Japan. She's with a robot. The robot is from Keihanna Science City near Kyoto. This robot can see and it can speak. It can move, but it can't run. It can carry things – for example, Nabeshima's basket.

Robots are amazing. They can help people in their lives.

Photo by Randy Olson

Reading

1 Look at the photo. Find:

two women	a robot	a child	a basket

2 Read the article. <u>Underline</u>:
1 the woman's name
2 four things this robot can do
3 one thing this robot can't do

Grammar *can/can't*

3 Choose the correct option to make a true sentence.

Robots *can / can't* help people.

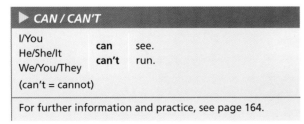

▶ **CAN / CAN'T**

I/You He/She/It We/You/They	can can't	see. run.
(can't = cannot)		

For further information and practice, see page 164.

4 Look at the example. Write sentences with *can* and *can't*.

Example:
robots / move ✓
Robots can move.

1 robots / speak ✓
2 robots / carry things ✓
3 people / fly ✗
4 I / speak English ✓
5 my grandfather / run ✗

5 Pronunciation *can/can't*

🔊 **1.69** Listen and check your sentences from Exercise 4. Then listen again and repeat.

Vocabulary **abilities**

6 💿 **1.70** Listen. Tick (✓) the sentences that are true for you. Make the other sentences negative.

1 I can cook. 2 I can speak English. 3 I can play table tennis. 4 I can drive a car.

5 I can ride a bike. 6 I can swim. 7 I can sing. 8 I can play the piano.

7 Work in pairs.

Student A: Read your sentences to your partner.

Student B: Write the number of the sentence. Then write ✓ (*can*) or ✗ (*can't*).

Take turns.

Listening

8 💿 **1.71** Listen to an interview with Christine Black, a robot expert. Are the sentences true (T) or false (F)?

1 The robot's name is Tomo.
2 Tomo is an American robot.
3 Tomo is from a new generation of robots.
4 'Tomo' is Japanese for 'intelligent'.

9 💿 **1.71** Listen again. What are the answers to the questions? Write ✓ (*can*) or ✗ (*can't*).

1 Can Tomo speak Japanese?
2 Can she sing?
3 Can she play the piano?
4 Can she swim?

Grammar *can* questions and short answers

10 Look at the grammar box. Write full answers to the questions in Exercise 9.

▶ CAN QUESTIONS and SHORT ANSWERS		
Can	I/you he/she/it we/you/they	speak Japanese? swim?
Yes, No,	I/you he/she/it we/you/they	can. can't.
For further information and practice, see page 164.		

Speaking

11 Work in pairs. Ask and answer questions about the abilities in Exercise 6.

Can you cook?

Yes, I can.

No, I can't.

5b Technology and me

Vocabulary **technology**

1 Look at the objects. Number the words (1–5).

> a camera   a video camera
> headphones   a webcam
> an MP3 player

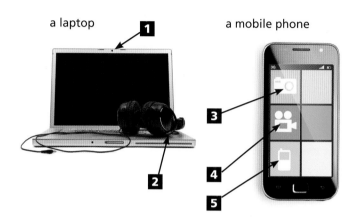

a laptop   a mobile phone

2 💿 **1.72** Listen and check your answers from Exercise 1.

Grammar *have/has*

3 Look at the grammar box. Then look at the
sentences. Choose the correct option.

1 This laptop *have* / *has* a webcam.
2 Mobile phones *have* / *has* MP3 players.

▶ HAVE/HAS		
I/You/We/You/They	**have**	a camera.
He/She/It	**has**	headphones.
For further information and practice, see page 164.		

4 Work in pairs. Tell your partner about your
laptop, mobile phone or computer.

> *I have a mobile phone. It has a camera.*

intelligent travel blog

We ask six travellers about their favourite
piece of technology. Here are their comments.

This is my 'mobile office'. These things are in my
backpack.
Posted by **Ian Walker**

I can take hundreds of photos with my new camera.
It has a big memory.
Posted by **Sacha Brown**

I have an old webcam, but it's OK. I can see and talk
to my family at home.
Posted by **Luis dos Santos**

I can work on the train with my laptop. It has a good
battery.
Posted by **Adela Law**

My phone has a fantastic video camera. I can take
great videos.
Posted by **Hon Yin**

My MP3 player is small and light.
It's in my bag all the time.
Posted by **Adam LeBlanc**

a **backpack (n)** /ˈbækpæk/

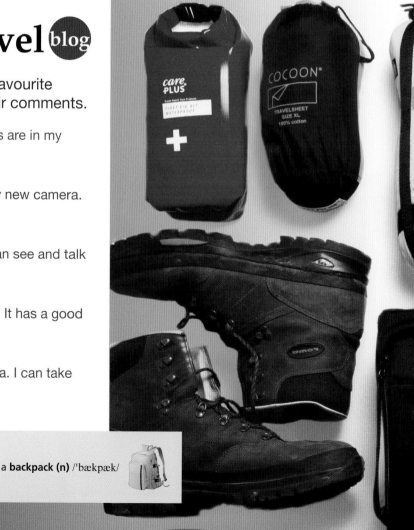

Reading

5 Work in pairs. Complete the sentences with objects from Exercise 1. Then read the comments in the *Intelligent Travel blog*. Which objects from your sentences are in the blog?

1 You can listen to music with ....
2 You can take photos with a ....
3 You can take videos with a ....
4 You can talk to people with a ....

6 Read the blog again. Find these adjectives. What do they describe?

> new   big   old   good   fantastic   great
> small   light

Grammar **adjective + noun**

7 Look at the words in **bold** in the grammar box. Circle the adjectives and <u>underline</u> the nouns.

> ▶ **ADJECTIVE + NOUN**
>
> My **camera** is **fantastic**.
> I have an **old webcam**.
>
> For further information and practice, see page 164.

8 Look at the example. Then write sentences.

Example:
This is my camera. It's new.
This is my new camera.

1 It's an MP3 player. It's new.
2 This is a laptop. It's fantastic.
3 My phone has a battery. The battery is small.
4 They are headphones. They are light.
5 I have a video camera. It's digital.

Writing and speaking

9 What's your favourite piece of technology? Write a comment for the *Intelligent Travel blog*.

10 Work in groups. Talk about your favourite piece of technology. Are your favourite pieces of technology the same – or different?

> What's your favourite piece of technology?
>
> My mobile phone.
>
> Why?
>
> It's new and it has a great camera.

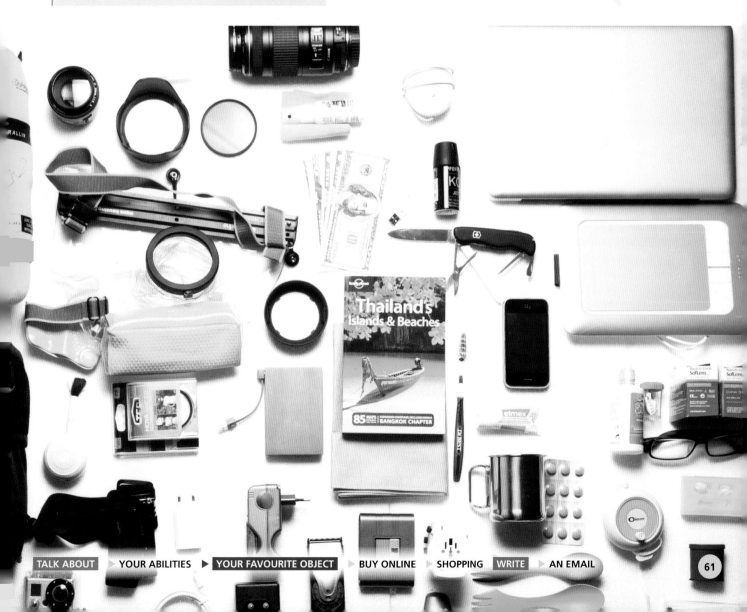

5c Solar ovens

Reading

1 Work in pairs. Match the words with the photos (1–3). Are these ovens popular in your country?

> an electric oven   a gas oven
> a microwave oven

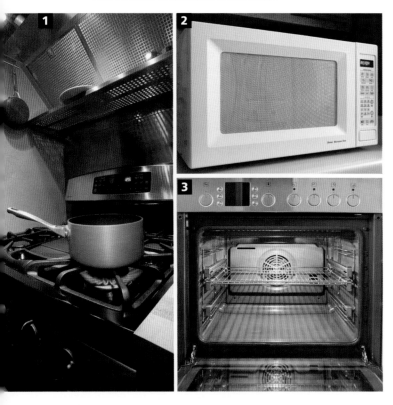

2 The article on page 63 is about solar ovens. Look at the photos and find:

> a box   a pot   newspaper

3 Read the article. Write this information for the two ovens.

	Bøhmer	HotPot
Number of parts		
Price		
Maximum temperature		

4 Read the article again. Are the sentences true (T) or false (F)?

1 Solar ovens can heat water.
2 You can buy the Bøhmer oven in shops.
3 The Bøhmer oven has five parts.
4 The HotPot oven has a glass bowl.
5 You can buy the HotPot oven online.

Grammar *very, really*

5 Look at the sentences in the grammar box. Which sentences are from the article?

> ▶ **VERY, REALLY**
>
> This oven is **very** basic.   This oven is **really** basic.
>
> It's **very** cheap.   It's **really** cheap!
>
> Note: really great ✓ really fantastic ✓
> BUT ~~very great~~ ✗ ~~very fantastic~~ ✗
>
> For further information and practice, see page 164.

6 Put the words in order to make sentences.

1 basic / this / is / design / very
2 basic / this / a / oven / is / really
3 very / solar ovens / are / cheap
4 is / a / designer / very / he / good
5 really / my / has / camera / big / a / memory
6 phone / this / really / a / has / good / video camera

7 Word focus *this*

a Match the sentences (1–4) with the pictures (a–d).

1 This is my <u>new</u> camera.
2 What's <u>this</u> in English?
3 This is my <u>sister</u> Anita.
4 Is the <u>Plaza Hotel</u> in this street?

b Work in pairs. Change the <u>underlined</u> words in the sentences in Exercise 7a.

> *This is my new phone.*   It's very nice.

Speaking

8 Work in pairs. Ask and answer questions about two microwave ovens.

Student A: Turn to page 154.

Student B: Turn to page 158.

T ECHNOLOGY

Solar ovens

People in some parts of the world can't cook with gas or electric ovens, but they can cook with the sun! Solar ovens are really fantastic. They can cook food and heat water. Here are two solar ovens.

The Bøhmer oven

This oven is very basic. The designer is Jon Bøhmer. He's Norwegian, but he lives in Kenya. You can't buy this oven, but you can make it. It has five parts: a lid, a pot, two boxes and newspaper. The total price of the parts is about $7. It's really cheap! The maximum temperature is about 90°C. This oven is very good for people in poor parts of the world.

The HotPot oven

The HotPot oven is a basic design too. It has three parts: a pot, a bowl and aluminium panels. The pot is in the glass bowl. The maximum temperature is about 150°C. It's really hot! You can buy this oven online and in shops. The price is about $100.

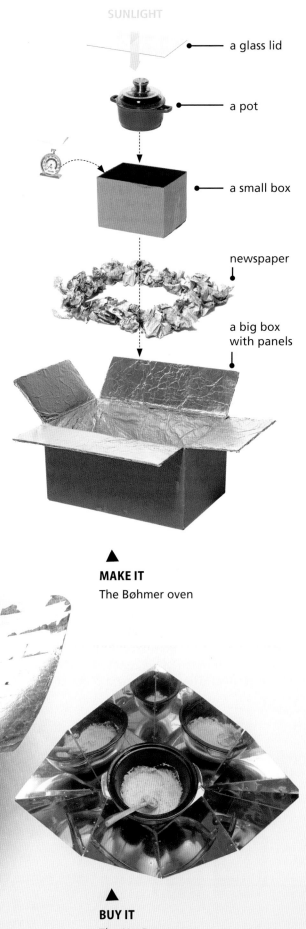

SUNLIGHT

- a glass lid
- a pot
- a small box
- newspaper
- a big box with panels

▲
MAKE IT
The Bøhmer oven

▲
BUY IT
The HotPot oven

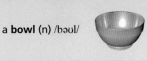

a **bowl** (n) /bəʊl/   the **sun** (n) /sʌn/

5d How much is it?

Vocabulary money and prices

1 Match the symbols with the money.

1 $ euros
2 £   pounds
3 €   dollars

2 Work in pairs. What's the money of these countries?

> Australia   Brazil   Canada   Egypt   Germany
> Ireland   Japan   the United Arab Emirates
> the United Kingdom   the United States

3 🎵 **1.73** Listen and repeat the prices.

4 Pronunciation **numbers**

a 🎵 **1.74** Listen and tick (✓) the correct price.

1	£13.00	£30.00	4	£16.00	£60.00
2	£14.00	£40.00	5	£17.00	£70.00
3	£15.00	£50.00	6	£18.00	£80.00

b 🎵 **1.74** Listen again and repeat the prices.

c Work in pairs. Take turns to dictate three prices to your partner.

Real life shopping

5 🎵 **1.75** Listen to three conversations in shops. Write the number of the conversation (1–3) next to the product. There is one extra product.

an alarm clock

memory sticks

speakers

a video camera

6 🎵 **1.75** Listen to the conversations again. Tick (✓) the correct price.

1	£15	£50	£80
2	£46.50	£65.60	£95.50
3	£5.99	£9.99	£99

7 Look at the expressions for SHOPPING. Write customer (C) or shop assistant (A).

> ▶ **SHOPPING**
>
> Excuse me.
> Can I help you?
> I'd like this video camera, please.
> How much is this alarm clock?
> How much are these memory sticks?
> It's / They're 50 pounds.
> That's £95.50, please.
> Can I pay with euros / cash / a card?
> Here you are.

8 Work in pairs. Look at the audioscript on page 171. Practise the conversations.

9 Work in pairs. Take turns to buy a product from your partner.

Shop assistant: Decide the price of the products.

Customer: Decide how much you can pay.

a digital camera

headphones

an MP3 player

a webcam

5e Can you help me?

Writing **an email**

1 Read the email and the reply. Answer the questions.

1 Who is Eliza?
2 Who is Mike?
3 What is Eliza's question?
4 What is Mike's answer?

2 Read Mike's reply again. Complete the table.

	Positive +	Negative –
Tablets	small, ... screens special pen	.... small screens
Laptops	.... screens keyboard	

Computer Life *Weekly*

can help with your IT questions.

Email mike@computerlifeweekly.com.

Hi Mike

I'm in my first term at college and I'd like a new computer. My PC is old and slow. I can buy a laptop or a tablet. I can't decide. Can you help me?

Eliza

Hi Eliza

Tablets are small and light, but they are expensive. Tablets have good screens, but they are small. Laptops have big screens. Can you type? Laptops have a keyboard. Tablets have a special pen and you can write on the screen. This is great, but it's slow. Good luck in your studies!

screen

keyboard

Mike, Computer Life Weekly

3 Writing skill *but*

a Look at the example. Then underline two sentences with *but* in Mike's reply.

Example: Tablets are small and light. They are expensive.
*Tablets are small and light, **but** they are expensive.*

b Read the pairs of sentences. Which pair can you not rewrite with *but*?

1 This tablet is great. It's expensive.
2 That book is old. It's interesting.
3 Tablet screens aren't big. They are good quality.
4 This computer is old. It's slow.
5 With this phone, you can watch videos. You can't edit videos.

c Rewrite four of the pairs of sentences with *but*.

4 Write a reply to this email. Before you write, make notes on the two things. Use a table.

> Hi Jo
>
> I'm in my first term at college. The bus to college is slow. I'd like a bike or a motorbike. I can't decide. Can you help me?
>
> Billie

5 Check your reply. Check the spelling, the capital letters and the use of *but*.

6 Work in pairs. Exchange replies. Is your partner's reply useful?

5f What's your favourite gadget?

People at a meeeting in the United States

Before you watch

1 Where can you find these gadgets? Use these words.

> a bag   a kitchen   an office

a camera

a coffee machine

a laptop

a memory stick

a microwave oven

a mobile phone

2 Work in pairs. Tell your partner the gadgets from Exercise 1 you have.

> *I have a microwave in my kitchen.*

> *I have a laptop in my office.*

3 🔊 **1.76**   Look at the word box. Listen and repeat the words.

4 In the video, an engineer and a doctor talk about their favourite gadgets. What do you think the gadgets are?

While you watch

5 Watch the video and check your ideas from Exercise 4.

6 Work in pairs. What can you remember about the two gadgets?

7 Watch again. Tick (✓) the options (a–d) you hear.

The engineer's favourite gadget ... .
a has a diary
b is expensive
c has a keyboard
d has a camera

The doctor's favourite gadget ... .
a is basic
b is Italian
c can make coffee in two minutes
d is in the office

8 Can you remember who says these things? Write engineer (E) or doctor (D). Then watch the video again and check.

1 _____ is very busy.
2 _____ has a new gadget.
3 _____ has a bad memory.
4 _____ has a lot of gadgets.
5 _____ can talk to the gadget.

9 Work in pairs. Read the sentences about each person's favourite gadget. Why do you think this gadget is their favourite? Choose the correct option (a or b).

The engineer:
a It's really important in his job.
b He can talk to it.

The doctor:
a Her machine isn't an expensive model.
b She can make coffee for her friends.

After you watch

10 Complete the information about the gadgets with the words.

> camera   email   friends   office
> phone   photos   photos

This phone has a great ¹ _____ . I can take fantastic ² _____ and I can send them to my ³ _____ or to the computer in my ⁴ _____ . The ⁵ _____ from this phone are really, really good! And I can talk to my ⁶ _____ ! I can say 'Send this photo to John.' or 'Send an ⁷ _____ to my office.' or 'Call home.'

> basic   coffee   expensive   friends
> kitchen   microwave   ten

Some coffee machines are ¹ _____ , but my new machine is a ² _____ machine and it isn't expensive. It's in my ³ _____ next to my ⁴ _____ . I have a lot of gadgets in my kitchen. I can make a cup of ⁵ _____ in two minutes. And it's fantastic coffee. I have ⁶ _____ different types of coffee! So I can make different types of coffee for my ⁷ _____ .

11 What's your favourite gadget? Why? Tell the class.

an **appointment** (n) /əˈpɔɪntmənt/ a meeting at a fixed time	a **kitchen** (n) /ˈkɪtʃən/
busy (adj) /ˈbɪzi/ 'I'm very busy today – I have six appointments!'	**organise** (v) /ˈɔːɡənaɪz/ to plan
a **gadget** (n) /ˈɡædʒɪt/ a piece of technology	

Grammar

1 Work in pairs. Ask and answer questions about Lynn. Use *can*. Take turns.

1	drive a car ✓	5	speak Arabic ✗
2	drive a motorbike ✗	6	speak Russian ✓
3	cook ✓	7	write in Arabic ✗
4	type ✓	8	write in Russian ✗

2 Work in pairs. Play a memory game. Take turns to make a sentence about Lynn.

3 Complete the text with these words.

's	fantastic	has	has	invention	really

This e-Reader has a ¹_____ big memory – it can store 1,400 books. It ²_____ small and light. It ³_____ a 15-hour battery. You can buy books online with this e-Reader. It ⁴_____ a keyboard on screen. E-readers are a ⁵_____ ⁶_____ .

I CAN	
talk about ability (*can*)	
talk about possessions and features (*have*)	
describe objects (adjective + noun)	
use *very* and *really* correctly	

Vocabulary

4 Match five of the verbs from A with words from B.

A	B
drive	a bike
play	a car
play	the piano
ride	three languages
speak	tennis

5 Write ✓ or ✗ next to the objects.

1 You can listen to music with:
  a phone   headphones   an MP3 player
2 You can take a photo with:
  speakers   a phone   a camera
3 You can speak to people with:
  a video camera   a laptop   a memory stick

6 Work in pairs. Tell your partner about the objects in Exercise 5.

> *I have a phone. It's in my bag.*

> *I have headphones. They're in my house.*

7 Work in pairs. Take turns.

Student A: Choose a price tag and say the price.

Student B: Point to the price tag.

$14.99   €50   £13.30   £71.40   €17.50 $19.90   €90.95   £45.70

I CAN	
talk about abilities	
talk about technology	
talk about money	

Real life

8 Complete the conversation between a customer (C) and a shop assistant (A) with these words. There is one extra word.

are	help	here	like	much	pay
that's	they're				

A: Can I ¹_____ you?
C: How ²_____ are these webcams?
A: ³_____ 27 euros.
C: OK. I'd ⁴_____ this webcam and a memory stick, please.
A: ⁵_____ you are. ⁶_____ 37.50, please.
C: Can I ⁷_____ with a card?
A: Yes, of course.

I CAN	
ask and talk about prices	
buy things in a shop	

Speaking

9 Work in pairs. Practise the conversation in Exercise 8. Change the objects and the prices.

Unit 6 Passions

Passionate sports fans in
Soweto, South Africa

FEATURES

1 🔘 **1.77** Look at the photo. What's the sport? Listen and check.

> basketball   football   rugby   tennis

2 🔘 **1.77** Look at these numbers. Then listen again and choose the correct option. Practise saying the numbers.

> 100 = one hundred   1,000,000 = one million
> 1,000 = one thousand

1 About 270 *thousand / million* people play football around the world.
2 Football is popular in more than two *hundred / thousand* countries.
3 The World Cup prize is 30 *thousand / million* US dollars.

3 Work in pairs. Take turns to say the numbers. Then dictate three numbers to your partner.

> | 300 | 9,000 | 20,000 | 70,000,000 |
> | 6,000,000 | 13,000,000 | 45,000 | 800 |

4 Work in groups. Answer the questions.

1 Which sports are popular in your country?
2 What's the national sport in your country?
3 What sports can you play?

6a A passion for vegetables

Reading

1 Look at the photo and the caption. What is Steve Weston's passion?

2 Read about Steve Weston. Answer the questions.

1 Where is Steve Weston in the photo?
2 What's the name of this kind of vegetable?
3 What is the weight of the vegetable in the photo?
4 Can you eat this vegetable?

Grammar *like*

3 Look at the grammar box. Then look at the article again. <u>Underline</u> the sentences with *like* and *don't like*.

▶ *LIKE*		
I/You/We/You/They	**like**	pumpkins.
	don't like	pumpkin pie.
(don't = do not)		

For further information and practice, see page 164.

Competitions for giant vegetables are popular here in the United States. This is my prize pumpkin!

A passion for vegetables

STEVE WESTON

Hi! My name's Steve Weston and I'm passionate about vegetables! Here I am in my garden with a giant pumpkin. I like pumpkins a lot because they can grow big. This pumpkin is about 700 kilograms. You can make a dish called pumpkin pie from pumpkins. It's a traditional dish in the United States. A lot of people like pumpkin pie, but I don't like it!

pumpkin pie (n)
/ˈpʌmpkɪn paɪ/

4 Look at the example. Then complete the sentences with *like* (☺) or *don't like* (☹).

Example:
I / vegetables. ☺
I like vegetables.

1 I / my garden. ☺
2 I / competitions. ☹
3 My friends / sports. ☺
4 I / football. ☹
5 We / tennis. ☺

5 🔊 **1.78** Listen and check your answers from Exercise 4. Then listen and repeat.

6 Change the sentences in Exercise 4 so they are true for you. Read the sentences to your partner.

> *I don't like vegetables.*

Vocabulary **food**

7 Look at the photos. Write these words with the photos.

> pasta   chocolate   vegetables   salad

cheese

_____

eggs

fish

fruit

meat

rice

_____

_____

8 🔊 **1.79** Listen and repeat the food words.

9 Work in pairs. Talk about the food in the photos.

> *I like cheese.*

> *I don't like cheese very much.*

Listening

10 🔊 **1.80** Listen to an interview with Steve. Tick (✓) the questions you hear.

1 Do you like fruit?   4 Do you like meat?
2 Do you like fruit pie?   5 Do you like pasta?
3 Do you like salad?

11 🔊 **1.80** Listen again. Choose the correct option: like (☺) or don't like (☹).

1 fruit   ☺ / ☹   4 meat   ☺ / ☹
2 fruit pie ☺ / ☹   5 pasta   ☺ / ☹
3 salad   ☺ / ☹

Grammar *like* questions and short answers

12 Look at the grammar box. What's the question form of *like*?

▶ *LIKE* QUESTIONS and SHORT ANSWERS			
Do	I/you/we/you/they	**like**	fruit?
Yes, No,	I/you/we/you/they	**do.** **don't.**	
For further information and practice, see page 164.			

13 Pronunciation *do you ... ?*

a 🔊 **1.81** Listen and repeat four questions from the interview.

b Work in pairs. Ask and answer the questions in Exercise 13a.

Speaking and writing

14 Prepare questions for a food survey. Write six questions with *Do you like ... ?*

15 Work in groups. Ask and answer the questions.

> *Alex, do you like pizza?*

> *Yes, I do.*

> *Krish, do you like pizza?*

> *No, I don't.*

16 Which foods are popular? Write sentences about your results. Compare with other groups.

> *In our group, three people like pizza.*

6b My favourite things

Vocabulary interests

1 🔊 **1.82** Look at the words in box A. Then look at the example. Match the words in box A with the pairs of words in box B. Then listen and check your answers.

Example:
birds, fish – animals

A
animals   books   films
music   sports   TV

B   jazz   pop
detective stories   novels
action films   comedies
birds   fish
reality shows   wildlife shows
scuba diving   swimming

2 Write your favourite TV show, book, film and sport.

TV show – Big Brother

3 Work in pairs. Ask and answer questions about the things in Exercise 2.

Do you like TV?

Yes, I do.

What's your favourite TV show?

Big Brother.

Reading

4 Read the article about Zeb Hogan. <u>Underline</u> four interests from Exercise 1.

5 Read the article again. Are the sentences true (T) or false (F)?

1 Zeb Hogan has two jobs.
2 He's a fisherman.
3 He's from Botswana.
4 His favourite sports are swimming and tennis.

My favourite things | Zeb Hogan

Name: Zeb Hogan
Place of Birth: Arizona
Current City: Reno, Nevada
Job: Research Professor,
University of Nevada and
TV presenter: *Monster Fish,*
Nat Geo TV

Grammar *he/she + like*

6 Look at the grammar box. Then look at the article. What is the negative form of *likes*?

▶ *HE/SHE + LIKE*			
He/She		**likes**	fish.
		doesn't like	cold places.
Does	he/she	**like**	coffee?
Yes,	he/she	**does.**	
No,		**doesn't.**	
(doesn't = does not)			
For further information and practice, see page 165.			

7 Look at the example. Write questions about Zeb Hogan.

Example:
like / fish?
Does he like fish?

1 like / Botswana?
2 like / Arizona?
3 like / cold places?
4 like / hot places?
5 like / coffee?

8 Work in pairs. Ask and answer the questions in Exercise 7 with *yes, no* or *I don't know.*

Zeb Hogan likes fish. His passion is giant fish. He isn't a fisherman. He's a scientist. His job is to study and protect giant fish in different places around the world – for example, in the Okavango Delta in Botswana. That's Zeb's favourite place. Zeb's from a big city in Arizona. It's a very hot, dry place. He doesn't like cold places. Does he like wet places? Well, he likes water! He loves swimming and scuba diving in his free time. Zeb's other passions are his friends and family, wildlife shows on TV … and coffee!

9 Write five sentences about Zeb Hogan. Use *likes / doesn't like.*

10 **Pronunciation** *likes, doesn't like*

a 🔊 1.83 Listen to five sentences about Zeb Hogan.

b 🔊 1.83 Listen again and repeat the sentences.

Speaking

11 Work in pairs. Look at the table.

Student A: Choose a person.

Student B: Ask *Does she like … ?* to discover the identity.

Take turns.

> *Does she like music?*

> *No, she doesn't.*

> *Does she like films?*

> *Yes, she does.*

> *Is it Teresa?*

> *Yes!*

	Barbara	Diana	Stella	Teresa
🐾	✓	✓	✗	✗
📖	✗	✗	✓	✓
🎞	✗	✓	✗	✓
🎵	✓	✗	✓	✗
👟	✗	✓	✗	✓
🖥	✓	✗	✓	✗

6c In love with speed

Reading

1 Work in pairs. Look at the photos. Can you name famous sports events with these things?

athletes
motorbikes
cars
boats
bicycles

2 Look at your answers from Exercise 1. Answer the questions for each event.

1 Which city or country is the race in?
2 What is the prize?
3 Can you name any famous winners of the event?

3 Look at the photos on page 75 and find these animals.

| a bird | a camel | a horse |

4 Read the article on page 75. Find:

1 three types of racing
2 five countries
3 two types of prize

5 Read the article again. Complete the sentences.

1 _____ racing is popular in China.
2 _____ racing is popular in Europe.
3 People in Qatar love _____ racing.
4 _____ can run at 65 kilometres per hour.
5 _____ can fly 100 to 1,000 kilometres.

6 Match the comments from three people with the sports.

1 'This sport is popular in Australia, but I don't like it.'
2 'My birds are special to me. I like them a lot!'
3 'My brother is in this race. I can see him on his horse.'

Grammar **object pronouns**

7 Look at the grammar box. Then look at the comments in Exercise 6. Find four object pronouns from the grammar box in the comments.

▶ OBJECT PRONOUNS	
Subject pronoun	**Object pronoun**
I	me
you	you
he	him
she	her
it	it
we	us
you	you
they	them

For further information and practice, see page 165.

8 Choose the correct option.

1 That's my horse. I love *them / it*.
2 He's fantastic. I like *him / her* a lot.
3 Australians are great. I like *them / him*.
4 Where's your sister? I can't see *her / you*.
5 The *Tour de France* is a great race. I like *her / it*.
6 Can I help *me / you*?

9 Word focus *it*

a Match 1–5 with a–e. Then <u>underline</u> *it* in the sentences.

1 What time is it?
2 Is it hot in your city today?
3 What's your favourite place?
4 What day is it?
5 Hello, 937 865.

a London. I love it.
b It's ten o'clock.
c It's Monday.
d Hi, it's Susan.
e No, it's cold.

b Work in pairs. Ask and answer questions 1–4.

Speaking

10 Work in pairs. Ask and answer questions about international sports events.

Student A: Turn to page 155

Student B: Turn to page 159

IN LOVE WITH SPEED

People love speed, racing and winning. Read about our passion for races.

THE LITANG HORSE FESTIVAL is in China. It's in the first week of August. The horses are small and fast. The races are over 300 kilometres. The prize is money or a special horse. People in China love this festival. It's a big tourist attraction.

Camel racing is a popular sport in Qatar. Camels are fast. Their top speed is about 65 kilometres per hour. They can run at 40 kilometres per hour over a long distance. Australians love camel racing too. One big race in Australia has prize money of $50,000.

Racing pigeons are birds. In a race, they can fly from 100 to 1,000 kilometres. Pigeon races are popular in Belgium and in the United Kingdom. A racing pigeon's top speed is about 130 kilometres per hour. It was a sport at the Paris Olympic games in 1900!

festival (n) /ˈfestɪvəl/ a special day or celebration
tourist attraction (n) /ˈtʊərɪst əˌtrækʃən/ people visit this interesting place

6d Let's play table tennis

Vocabulary opinion adjectives

1 🎵 **1.84** Listen to three conversations (1–3). Match the words from the conversations with the four opinion adjectives.

a   Emily Blunt
b   sport
c   pasta
d   pizza

boring

horrible

fantastic / great

2 Are the adjectives in Exercise 1 positive (+) or negative (-)? Write them in the table.

Positive +	Negative −

3 Pronunciation intonation

🎵 **1.85** Listen and repeat the opinions from the conversations.

4 Work in pairs. Add the names of four people or things to the list in Exercise 1. Tell your partner your opinion.

> *Basketball's boring.*

Real life suggestions

5 🎵 **1.84** Complete the conversations with the expressions for making and responding to SUGGESTIONS. Then listen again and check.

1
A: Let's watch TV tonight.
B: _____ . What's on?
A: A film with Emily Blunt is on at eight o'clock.
B: Oh, _____ . She's fantastic.

2
A: _____ .
B: _____ . I don't like table tennis.
A: OK. _____ .
B: Sorry. Sport's boring.

3
A: Let's have pasta this weekend.
B: _____ . It's horrible.
A: _____ . How about pizza? Do you like pizza?
B: Yes, it's great.

▶ **SUGGESTIONS**

Let's play table tennis tomorrow.	How about football?
That's a good idea.	No, thanks.
I love her.	I don't like pasta.
	OK.

---

6 Add three ideas to the table below.

Let's	play have watch	a film an action film curry football pasta pizza table tennis tennis TV _____ _____ _____	tonight. tomorrow. this weekend.
How about		… ?	

7 Work in pairs. Take turns to make suggestions and respond with opinions.

8 Work in a group. Make suggestions and agree on an activity for this weekend.

TALK ABOUT   ▶ A FOOD SURVEY   ▶ THINGS IN COMMON   ▶ A SPORTS EVENT   ▶ SUGGESTIONS   WRITE   ▶ A REVIEW

6e A fantastic film

Writing **a review**

1 Read the reviews (1 and 2). Match the reviews with two of the pictures (a–c).

1 ⬛ review

★ ★ ★ ★ ★

This is a fantastic film. I love it! The star is Matt Damon. I love him too! He's great in this film.

Peter Black (UK)

2 ⬛ review

★ ★ ★ ★ ★

This is a great book. The writer is Zadie Smith. She's my favourite writer. I have all of her books. I really like them.

Eli (Ireland)

2 Read the reviews again. Complete the tables.

Film title	
Star	
Name of reviewer	
Reviewer's opinion	

Book title	
Writer	
Name of reviewer	
Reviewer's opinion	

3 Writing skill **pronouns**

a Read about film b in Exercise 1. Use four of these pronouns to complete the review.

he	him	it	she	she	them	her

This is a great film. I love ¹ _____ ! The star is Emily Blunt. I love ² _____ . ³ _____ 's my favourite film star! ⁴ _____ 's fantastic in this film.

b Complete these sentences with the correct pronoun.

1 'Do you like Matt Damon's films?'
  'Yes, I love _____ .'
2 Russell Crowe is in this film. _____ 's great.
3 'Meryl Streep is my favourite film star.'
  'I don't like _____ very much.'
4 'I like Zadie Smith's books.'
  'I like _____ too.'
5 'This film is boring.'
  'Oh! I like _____ .'
6 This is a good book. _____ 's fantastic.

4 Write a review for a book or film you like.

5 Check your review. Check the pronouns and the spelling.

6 Work in pairs. Exchange your reviews. Do you agree with your partner's opinion?

6f At the market

THE COVERED M
Fifty Quality Indeper

Helen & Douglas House

Price's Pet Supplies

Ben's Cookies

NEW TAKEAWAY
MEAL DEAL!
3 FOR
£3.33
Any baguette
+
Hot or
cold drink
+
Fruit or
crisps
3 FOR
£3.33

At the Covered Market in Oxford

Before you watch

1 Look at the photos. Write the names with the market stalls.

> a cheese stall   a fish stall
> a fruit and vegetable stall

2 🎵 **1.86**   Look at the word box. Listen and repeat the words.

3 Look at the word box again. Find four things you can buy at the stalls in Exercise 1.

4 Work in pairs. Say things you can buy at a market. Take turns. How many things can you say in 30 seconds?

While you watch

5 Watch the video and write the number (1–3) next to the question.

    a   Which stalls do you like?
    b   Is this your local market?
    c   Tell us what you don't like.

6 Work in pairs. What can you remember? How many things in your list from Exercise 4 are in the video?

7 Read the sentences. Then watch the video again and choose the correct option (a–c).

    1   Jan Szafranski … .
        a   likes the fruit and vegetable stall
        b   likes the cheese stall
        c   likes the fish stall

    2   Amy Miller … .
        a   doesn't like fruit
        b   doesn't like vegetables
        c   doesn't like meat

    3   Richard Lewis … .
        a   loves English cheese
        b   loves French cheese
        c   loves tomatoes

8 Watch the video again. Are the sentences true (T) or false (F)?

    1   Richard's school is near the market.
    2   Amy's favourite stall is the cheese stall.
    3   Jan can cook fish.

9 What can you remember? Who says these sentences? Write the name of the person.

    1   My house is in this street, so this is my local market.
    2   Yes, this is my local market. And it's really great.
    3   My wife likes it, but I don't. It has bones. I don't like them.
    4   I can't think – maybe tomatoes. I don't like them very much.
    5   I'm a vegetarian.

After you watch

10 Work in pairs. Take turns to buy things from your partner.

Student A: You are in the market. Write your shopping list.

Student B: You have a stall in the market. Decide what you sell and the prices.

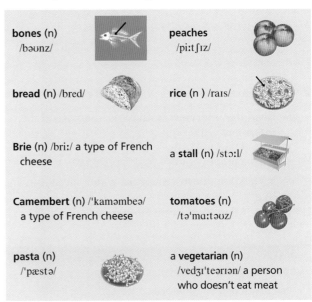

bones (n) /bəʊnz/	**peaches** /piːtʃɪz/
bread (n) /bred/	**rice** (n) /raɪs/
Brie (n) /briː/ a type of French cheese	**a stall** (n) /stɔːl/
Camembert (n) /ˈkaməmbeə/ a type of French cheese	**tomatoes** (n) /təˈmaːtəʊz/
pasta (n) /ˈpæstə/	**a vegetarian** (n) /vedʒɪˈteərɪən/ a person who doesn't eat meat

UNIT 6 REVIEW

Grammar

1 Complete the article about Kirk Allen with the correct form of *like*.

Explore Travel

Kirk Allen is passionate about scuba diving. It's his job. He [1]_____ it very much. But [2]_____ cold water? [3]_____ boats? And what are his free-time interests? Read our interview with Kirk and find out.

Kirk, you are a professional scuba diver. Why?
Well, I [4]_____ swimming and scuba diving. And I love the sea.

[5]_____ *the water?*
Yes and no. I [6]_____ very cold water very much. It isn't very nice.

Is this your boat?
Yes, it is. I have three boats. I [7]_____ big boats. They're fantastic!

And finally, what are your free-time interests?
I [8]_____ sports. And I love action films too.

2 Complete the sentences with object pronouns.

1 Read the interview with Kirk Allen. Read the interview with _____ .
2 Kirk Allen loves the sea. He loves _____ .
3 Kirk Allen likes big boats. He likes _____ .
4 Kirk Allen doesn't like cold water. He doesn't like _____ .
5 Kirk Allen likes Anne Hathaway's films. He likes _____ .

I CAN	
talk about likes and dislikes (*like*)	
use object pronouns correctly	

Vocabulary

3 Add the vowels and write the words. Then look at the shopping basket and tick (✓) the things.

1 mt _____
2 chs _____
3 sld _____
4 vgtbls _____
5 fsh _____
6 frt _____
7 rc _____
8 ggs _____
9 pst _____
10 chclt _____

4 Underline the odd one out in each group.

1 tennis   football   chocolate
2 swimming   pop   jazz
3 comedies   birds   action films
4 camels   basketball   fish
5 horses   novels   detective stories
6 scuba diving   rugby   reality shows

5 How many examples can you find in Exercise 4 for these words?

1 music   3 animals   5 TV
2 sports   4 films   6 books

6 Choose the correct option.

1 I like Adele. She's *fantastic / horrible*.
2 I don't like pigeons. They're *great / horrible*.
3 I love jazz. It's *boring / great*.
4 'Do you like reality shows?'
   'No, I don't. They're *boring / fantastic*.'

I CAN	
talk about food	
talk about interests	
give positive and negative opinions (adjectives)	

Real life

7 Read the conversation. Choose the correct option.

A: Let's *have curry / watch a film / play tennis* tonight.
B: That's a good idea. What's on?
A: A film with Will Smith.
B: Oh, *it's horrible / I don't like him / she's fantastic*.
A: How about Zoe Saldana? I have her new DVD.
B: *No, thanks. / OK. Great. / Yes, it's great.*

I CAN	
give my opinion	
make and respond to suggestions	

Speaking

8 Work in pairs. Practise the conversation in Exercise 7 with the other two options.

Unit 7 Different lives

The festival of colours – the Holi festival – in Kolkata, India
Photo by Dibyangshu Sarkar

FEATURES

1 Look at the photo and the caption. Answer the questions.

1 Where are the people?
2 What is the celebration?

2 🔊 **2.1** Work in pairs. Listen to information about the Holi festival. Choose the correct option.

1 The Holi festival is in *December / March*.
2 It's a celebration of *new life / family life*.
3 The festival is one or two *days / weeks*.

3 🔊 **2.2** The Holi festival is a celebration of spring. Look at these words for the four seasons. Listen and repeat the words.

spring   summer   autumn   winter

4 Work in pairs. Which months are the seasons in your country?

I'm from Peru. Winter is June, July and August.

7a The Sami people

Reading

1 Look at the two photos. What season is it?

2 Look at the photos and read the captions. Find:

> snow   a sledge   reindeer

3 Read the article about the Sami people. Find:

1. four countries
2. an animal
3. a language

a Henrik Gaup and one of his reindeer

b Sami people at a winter camp

The Sami people

By Jessica Benko
Photos by Franz Aberham

Henrik Gaup and his family are Sami. The Sami people live in Norway, Sweden, Finland and Russia. They are the 'people of the reindeer'. Henrik Gaup is a traditional Sami. 'I have five children,' he says. 'I teach my children about the reindeer. They don't study with books.' Henrik and his family speak Sami, but many Sami children don't understand it. Reindeer are very important to the Sami people. In the Sami language the word for 'a group of reindeer' is eallu and the word for 'life' is eallin.

4 Underline these words in the article. Then complete the sentences with two of the words.

| live | have | teach | speak |

1 The Sami people _____ in Norway, Sweden, Finland and Russia.
2 They _____ the Sami language.

5 Write two sentences for you. Read your sentences to your partner.

> *I live in Lima.*

Grammar present simple *I/you/we/you/they*

6 Look at the grammar box. Then look at this sentence. Choose the correct option. What is the negative form of the present simple?

Many Sami children *understand / don't understand* Sami.

▶ PRESENT SIMPLE *I/YOU/WE/YOU/THEY*	
I/You/We/You/They	**live** in Sweden. **don't study** with books.
For further information and practice, see page 165.	

7 🔊 **2.3** Read about traditional and modern Sami people. Choose the correct option. Then listen and check.

The traditional Sami [1] *live / understand* reindeer. In summer, they [2] *have / live* in traditional tents. They [3] *have / study* tractors. Today many young Sami [4] *live / teach* in modern homes. They [5] *have / speak* television and the Internet. They [6] *don't speak / don't understand* traditional Sami life.

| a **tent** /tent/ | a **tractor** /'træktə/ |

8 Pronunciation *don't*

a 🔊 **2.4** Listen and repeat four sentences.

b Are you different from the traditional Sami? Write three sentences with *don't*. Read your sentences to your partner.

> *I don't live in Sweden.*
> *They don't speak Spanish.*

9 Are these sentences true for you? Change them so they are true.

1 I don't live in a house.
2 I don't have three children.
3 I speak four languages.
4 I don't understand French.
5 I teach English.
6 I study with books.

Speaking and writing

10 Work in pairs. Find three things you have in common. Write sentences with *We*. You can use these verbs.

| have | live | speak | study |
| teach | understand | | |

> *I live in a house.*

> *I live in a flat.*

> *I speak English.*

> *I speak English too.*

We both speak English.

7b School life

Vocabulary **education**

1 Look at the photo. Match seven of these words with things and people in the photo.

> board   book   classmate   classroom
> college   pen   pencil   school   student
> teacher   university

2 Work in pairs. Look at the photo. Use some words from Exercise 1 to make sentences.

> *It isn't a university.*

> *No, it's a school.*

Kakenya Ntaiya is from a small village in Kenya. She's a Maasai. Kakenya is an unusual Maasai woman. She has a PhD from an American university. Now Kakenya is at home, in Kenya. She's a teacher. This is her school.

Maasai (n) /'mɑːsaɪ/ people from a part of East Africa
unusual (adj) /ʌnˈjuːʒəl/ different, not usual
village (n) /ˈvɪlɪdʒ/ a very small town

School life in Kenya

3 Use words from Exercise 1 to make true sentences for you.

1 I study / don't study at a …
2 I like my …
3 I have of lot of …

Reading and listening

4 Work in pairs. Read about Kakenya Ntaiya. Answer the questions.

1 Is she from America?
2 Is she a girl?
3 Is she a student?

5 🔊 2.5 Read these questions from an interview with a teacher at the school. Match the questions (1–5) with the answers (a–e). Then listen and check.

1 Do you work at Kakenya's school?
2 Do boys study at the school?
3 Do the girls live with their families?
4 Do they go home in summer?
5 Do the girls learn English at the school?

a No, they don't. The school is for girls.
b No, they don't. They live at the school.
c Yes, they do. They go home to their villages.
d Yes, they do. And in summer we teach extra classes in English too.
e Yes, I do. I teach there. We have five teachers.

6 Work in pairs. Do you think this school is unusual? Why? / Why not?

Grammar present simple questions *I/you/we/you/they*

7 Look at the grammar box. Then look at the questions in Exercise 5. <u>Underline</u> the question forms.

▶ PRESENT SIMPLE QUESTIONS *I/YOU/WE/ YOU/THEY*		
Do	I/you/we/you/they	**study** English?
Yes, No,	I/you/we/you/they	**do.** **don't.**
For further information and practice, see page 165.		

8 🔊 2.6 Put the words in order to make questions. Then listen to an interview with a student and check. Write (✓) or (✗) for his answers.

1 study / you / at a college / do / ?
2 classes / do / have / you / every day / ?
3 like / you / do / your classes / ?
4 you / do / live / near your university / ?
5 do / with your family / live / you / ?
6 you / go home / in the holidays / do / ?

9 Pronunciation **intonation in questions**

a 🔊 2.7 Listen and repeat the questions from Exercise 8.

b Work in pairs.

Student A: You are the interviewer.

Student B: You are Carl.

Ask and answer the questions. Take turns.

Writing and speaking

10 Prepare questions for a survey. Use these verbs. Choose an option for each question.

have	like	live	study

1 _____ at university? / at a language school? / online?
2 _____ with friends? / with classmates?
3 _____ classes in the morning? / classes in the afternoon? / classes in the evening?
4 _____ near your school? / near your college?
5 _____ your book? / your classroom?

11 Work in pairs. Take turns to ask and answer your questions.

Do you live with friends?

No, I don't. I live with my family.

7c A year in British Columbia, Canada

Vocabulary **weather**

1 🔊 **2.8** Look at the pictures. Listen and repeat the words.

cloudy   rainy   snowy

sunny   windy

2 🔊 **2.9** Listen to people from four places. Write the number (1–4) next to the weather word.

3 🔊 **2.9** Listen again. Match the speaker with the country and the season.

	Country	Season
1	Australia	autumn
2	Canada	spring
3	Great Britain	summer
4	South Africa	winter

4 Work in pairs. Describe the weather for seasons in your country.

> *I'm from India. Winter is the dry season. It's hot and sunny.*

Reading

5 Look at the photos on page 87 and find:

> flowers   ice   leaves   trees

6 Read the article on page 87. Match the paragraphs with the photos (a–d).

7 Read the article again. Find one thing the writer does in each season.

8 Underline the things people do in each season.

9 Do people in your country do the things in the article? Tell your partner.

> *We don't go skiing in winter.*

10 Word focus *go*

a Look at these expressions with *go*. Find four of them in the article on page 87.

> go to the beach   go to work   go home
> go swimming   go for walks

b Underline the option that is true for you.

1 I *go / don't go* to the beach in summer.
2 I *go / don't go* swimming in winter.
3 I *go / don't go* home in the evening.
4 I *go / don't go* to work every day.
5 I *go / don't go* for walks with my family.

Grammar **present simple with question words**

11 Look at the grammar box. Then look at the article. Find three of the question words from the grammar box in the article.

▶ PRESENT SIMPLE WITH QUESTION WORDS			
What			do?
Where			go?
Who	do	I/you/we/you/they/people	go with?
Why			go to the beach?
When			eat?

For further information and practice, see page 165.

12 Complete the questions with *what, where, who, why* and *when*.

1 _____ do you go in summer?
2 _____ do you do in autumn?
3 _____ do flowers open?
4 _____ do you go cycling with?
5 _____ do you like winter?

Speaking

13 Work in pairs. What's your favourite season? Ask and answer questions. Use these ideas.

- Why / like … ?
- What / do?
- When / do … ?
- Where / go?
- Who / go with?

> *My favourite season is winter.*   *Why do you like winter?*

> *I like cold weather.*

A YEAR IN BRITISH COLUMBIA, CANADA

By Chuck Spender

SUMMER

Where do people go in summer?

Summer is a great time for holidays here. The weather is hot and sunny. People go to the beach. They cook and eat outside. I go to Vancouver Island with my family. We play summer sports and we go swimming in lakes and rivers.

AUTUMN

What do people do in autumn?

In autumn, classes start. Children go to school. Students go to university. People go to work. It's cloudy and rainy. Trees change colour from green to brown. I think it's a beautiful season. I take a lot of photos in autumn.

WINTER

Where do people go in winter?

In winter, it's cold, rainy and snowy too. A lot of people stay at home. They watch TV, read books and cook winter food. Winter is my favourite season. I like winter sports. I go to Whistler. It's in the mountains. I go skiing and climbing. It's very cold!

SPRING

Why do people like spring?

For a lot of people, spring is their favourite season. The temperatures go up. It's cloudy and rainy, but it isn't cold. Flowers open, birds sing and trees are green. People go cycling and running. They meet friends and they go for walks. I play golf with my friends.

7d What's the matter?

Summer holidays in Great Britain

Vocabulary problems

1 🔊 **2.10** Look at the pictures and listen to seven people. Write the number (1–7) next to the picture.

a bored

b cold

c hot

d hungry

e thirsty

f tired

g wet

2 🔊 **2.11** Listen and repeat the expressions from Exercise 1.

3 Work in pairs. How do you feel right now? Tell your partner.

I'm hungry!

Real life problems

4 Work in pairs. Look at the photo. Describe the weather. Describe the people.

5 🔊 **2.12** Listen to the conversation. Write the names (F =father, P= Paul, A= Anna).

1 .... is thirsty.
2 .... doesn't feel well.
3 .... is cold and wet.
4 .... is bored.

6 🔊 **2.12** Listen again. Complete the mother's suggestions.

1 Why don't you have .... ?
2 Why don't you eat .... ?
3 Why don't you go .... ?

> ▶ **PROBLEMS**
>
> What's the matter?
> I'm hungry/thirsty/cold/tired/hot/wet/bored.
> It's cold/wet/hot.
> I don't feel well.
> I don't like swimming.
> I don't understand.
> Why don't you have cup of tea?

7 Pronunciation sentence stress

🔊 **2.13** Listen and repeat three sentences. Is *don't* stressed or unstressed?

8 Work in pairs. Look at the vocabulary in Exercise 1 and the expressions for talking about PROBLEMS. Take turns to talk about problems and make suggestions.

What's the matter?

I'm bored.

Why don't you read a book?

7e Photography club members

Writing **a profile**

1 Read Hans's profile. Are the sentences true (T) or false (F)?

1 Hans is a student.
2 He's married.
3 He's in a photography club.

2 Writing skill **paragraphs**

a Read Hans's profile again. Write the number of the paragraph.

a interests: ....
b professional information: ....
   ....
c family/friends: ....

b Read the profile information for Jenna. Number the paragraphs (a–c) in the correct order (1–3).

c Read the notes for Luther. Organise the notes into three paragraphs. Then write sentences with the words.

> Luther
> animals
> a teacher
> engineering
> City College
> my wife and children
> photos

3 Make notes about yourself for a profile. Are you in a club or a member of an organisation?

• professional information
• family/friends
• interests

4 Use your notes and write three paragraphs.

5 Check your profile. Check the paragraph order, the spelling and the punctuation.

6 Work in pairs. Exchange profiles. Find two things you and your partner have in common.

HANS

PLT Photography club members

1 I'm an engineer. I work at PLT Engineering.
2 I'm married and I have three children. We live in a small village near my company.
3 I like photography. I'm in the PLT photography club. In winter, we meet on Sunday. We go out and take photos. In summer, I go on holiday with my family. I take a lot of photos of my children and the places we go to.

JENNA

PLT Photography club members

a I live with three classmates. We live near our college.
b I like sports and photography. I take photos of sports people.
c I'm a student. I study engineering. I go to the City College. In the summer holidays, I work at PLT Engineering.

TALK ABOUT ▶ YOU AND YOUR PARTNER ▶ A SURVEY ▶ ACTIVITIES IN DIFFERENT SEASONS ▶ WHAT'S THE MATTER?

WRITE ▶ A PROFILE

89

7f The people of the reindeer

A Sami man with his reindeer

Before you watch

1 Work in pairs. Look at the photo on page 90. Answer the questions.

1 What kind of animals are they?
2 Who are the 'people of the reindeer'?
3 Where are they from?

2 🔊 **2.14** Look at the word box. Listen and repeat the words.

3 Work in pairs. What can you remember about the Sami people's lives? Are these sentences true (T) or false (F)?

1 They live in big cities.
2 They speak a traditional language.
3 They have modern homes.

4 Write three things you think are in the video.

While you watch

5 Watch the video and check your ideas from Exercise 4.

6 These things are in the video. Watch the video again and put the pictures in order.

a

a cup of coffee

b

a dog

c

a fire

d

snow *1*

e

a tent

f

a woman

g

a young child

h

a young couple

7 Read these sentences about the Sami. Tick (✓) the things you can see in the video.

1 The Sami travel on tractors.
2 When they travel with the reindeer, the Sami cook their food on a fire.
3 Some young people wear traditional clothes.
4 Reindeer meat and bread are traditional Sami foods.
5 Reindeer eat food under the snow.
6 The Sami people have dogs.

8 Watch Nils Peder Gaup in the last part of the video. Answer this question: what type of snow is good for the reindeer?

After you watch

9 Complete the paragraph with verbs. You can use the same verb more than once.

The Sami ¹_____ in Norway, Sweden, Finland and Russia. The reindeer ²_____ in spring. The Sami people ³_____ with them. On the journey, the people ⁴_____ in tents. These Sami people ⁵_____ traditional lives. The children ⁶_____ with the reindeer too.

10 Work in pairs.

Student A: You are from a Sami family. Choose your age – young or old.

Student B: You are a journalist.

Ask and answer questions with *when, where, what, who* and *why* about Sami life.

Take turns.

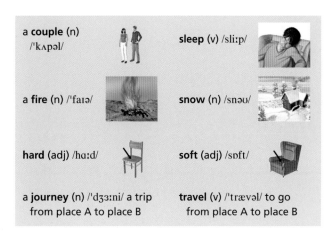

a **couple** (n) /ˈkʌpəl/

sleep (v) /sliːp/

a **fire** (n) /ˈfaɪə/

snow (n) /snəʊ/

hard (adj) /hɑːd/

soft (adj) /sɒft/

a **journey** (n) /ˈdʒɜːni/ a trip from place A to place B

travel (v) /ˈtrævəl/ to go from place A to place B

UNIT 7 REVIEW

Grammar

1 Read about Cathy Gulpilil. <u>Underline</u> two places and circle two languages in the article.

Cathy Gulpilil and her husband Albert are from the Northern Territory of Australia. Now they live in Sydney. They have two children. Cathy and Albert teach at a college. They speak English and Yirram – their parents' language. Cathy's and Albert's parents live in the Northern Territory. They don't like Sydney very much. Cathy and Albert's children understand Yirram, but they don't speak it.

2 Write the questions.

1 where / Cathy and Albert / live?
2 they / have / children?
3 where / they / teach?
4 they / speak / their parents' language?
5 their parents / like / Sydney?
6 their children / speak Yirram?

3 Work in pairs. Ask and answer the questions in Exercise 2. Take turns.

4 Work in pairs. Take turns.

Student A: You are Cathy or Albert Gulpilil.

Student B: Interview your partner. Use *you* and the questions in Exercise 2.

I CAN	
describe permanent states (present simple)	
ask and answer questions about habits (present simple)	

Vocabulary

5 Complete the words about education.

1 People: classmate, st _ _ _ _ _, te _ _ _ _ _
2 Places: college, un _ _ _ _ _ _ _ _, sc _ _ _ _,
   cl _ _ _ _ _ _ _
3 Things: board, bo _ _, pe _

6 Complete the sentences with these verbs. There is one extra verb.

have	like	live	play	speak	study
understand					

1 My friends _____ engineering at college.
2 I _____ in a small town.
3 'Do you _____ Arabic?'
   'No, I don't, but I _____ some words.'
4 My parents don't _____ a TV.
5 I _____ summer.

7 Complete the sentences with weather words.

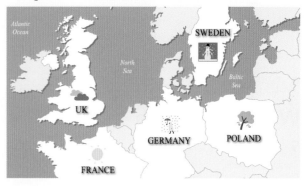

1 It's _____ in the UK.
2 It's _____ in France.
3 It's _____ in Sweden.
4 It's _____ in Poland.
5 It's _____ in Germany.

I CAN	
talk about education	
talk about people's lives	
talk about the weather	

Real life

8 Match words in A and B to make sentences. Then put the sentences in order to make a conversation.

	A	B
1	I'm	No thanks. _____ cold.
2	It's	the matter?
3	What's	eat this pizza?
4	Why don't you	hungry.

I CAN	
talk about problems	
make suggestions	

Speaking

9 Work in pairs. Practise the conversation in Exercise 8 with these ideas. Take turns to start.

1 thirsty / cup of coffee
2 hot / drink of water
3 don't understand / use a dictionary
4 bored / go for a walk

Unit 8 Routines

Farmers and wild horses
Photo by Melissa Farlow

FEATURES

94 Day and night

Routines at home and at work

96 A typical day

Two *National Geographic* explorers

98 Cats in crisis

A job in tiger conservation

102 The elephants of Samburu

A video about wildlife in Africa

1 Work in pairs. Look at the photo. Where do you think this is?

2 🔊 **2.15** Read the sentences about the man in the photo. Which option do you think is correct? Listen and check your ideas.

1 His job is *in an office / outside*.
2 Farmers *use / don't use* mobile phones.
3 They use *tractors / helicopters*.

3 Make true sentences about these jobs.

Artists Doctors Drivers Engineers Filmmakers Photographers Scientists Teachers Writers	work	outside. in laboratories. in offices. in schools. in studios. in hospitals. with people. with children. with animals. with modern technology.

4 Work in pairs. Take turns to choose a job from Exercise 3.

What do you do?

I work in a hospital.

You're a doctor.

8a Day and night

Vocabulary routines

1 Match the sentences (1–7) with the pictures (a–h).

1 I get up at ___six o'clock___ .   *f*
2 I have breakfast at _____ .
3 I start work at _____ .
4 I have lunch in a _____ .
5 I finish work at _____ .
6 I have dinner at _____ .
7 I go to bed at _____ .

2 🎵 **2.16** Listen and complete the sentences in Exercise 1 with times and places.

3 Work in pairs. Write seven true or false sentences about your routines. Read the sentences to your partner. Find your partner's false sentences.

Reading and listening

4 Look at the photo. Where is it? What kind of class is this?

5 Read about one of the women in the photo. Is her routine similar to your routine?

6 🎵 **2.17** Read the article again and listen. <u>Underline</u> the information that is different.

DAY AND NIGHT

A writer in China

Chen Hong is from Shanghai. She's a writer. She gets up at six o'clock in the morning. She doesn't have breakfast. She goes to an exercise class. The class is on the Bund, near the river. It starts at 7.15 and it finishes at 7.45. Then Chen has breakfast with her friends. She starts work at 8.30. She works at home. At midday, she has lunch. She finishes work at 6.30 in the evening. At eight o'clock, she has dinner with her family. She goes to bed at 10.30. Chen Hong doesn't work every day, but she goes to her exercise class every day.

A morning exercise class on the Bund (riverside) in Shanghai

Grammar present simple *he/she/it*

7 Look at the grammar box. Then <u>underline</u> the present simple verbs in the article about Chen Hong.

▶ PRESENT SIMPLE *HE/SHE/ IT*	
He/She/It	**gets up** at six o'clock. **doesn't have** breakfast. **starts** at 7.15.

For further information and practice, see page 166.

8 Complete the text about an astronomer with the correct form of the verbs.

finish	get up	go	go	have	have	not / work
start	work	work				

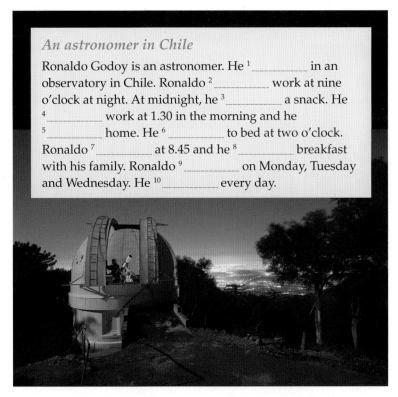

An astronomer in Chile

Ronaldo Godoy is an astronomer. He ¹_____ in an observatory in Chile. Ronaldo ²_____ work at nine o'clock at night. At midnight, he ³_____ a snack. He ⁴_____ work at 1.30 in the morning and he ⁵_____ home. He ⁶_____ to bed at two o'clock. Ronaldo ⁷_____ at 8.45 and he ⁸_____ breakfast with his family. Ronaldo ⁹_____ on Monday, Tuesday and Wednesday. He ¹⁰_____ every day.

Grammar prepositions of time

9 Look at the expressions in the grammar box. <u>Underline</u> similar expressions in the text in Exercise 8.

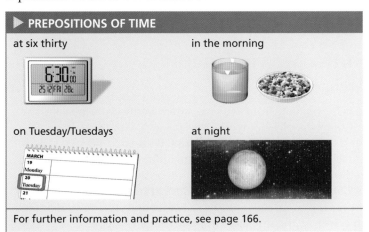

▶ PREPOSITIONS OF TIME	
at six thirty	in the morning
on Tuesday/Tuesdays	at night

For further information and practice, see page 166.

10 Pronunciation -*s* and -*es* verbs

a 🔊 **2.18** Listen and repeat the sentences with these verbs.

works	starts	finishes	goes
gets up			

b 🔊 **2.18** Listen again and look at the verbs. <u>Underline</u> the verb with an extra syllable.

work	start	finish	go	get up
works	starts	finishes	goes	gets up

Speaking and writing

11 Work as a class. Ask questions. Find one name for each sentence. You have a time limit of five minutes.

Find a person in your class who ...

gets up at six o'clock. ....

doesn't work. ....

has eggs for breakfast. ....

works in the evening. ....

doesn't have lunch. ....

goes to bed after midnight. ....

starts work at nine o'clock. ....

gets up late at the weekend. ....

Do you get up at six o'clock, Issa?

No, I don't. I get up at 7.15.

Do you get up at six o'clock, Leonardo?

Yes, I do.

12 Write sentences with the names.

Leonardo gets up at six o'clock.

8b A typical day

Reading

1 Look at the photos (1 and 2) and the captions. Read the sentences and write A (archaeologists), G (geologists) or B (both).

1 They work on archaeological sites.
2 They work outside.
3 They study rocks.
4 They study old objects.

2 Work in pairs. What do you think is the daily routine of the people in the photos?

3 Read about a geologist and an archaeologist, and check your ideas from Exercise 2.

2 Geologists at work near the Azores, Atlantic Ocean

1 Archaeologists on a site in Canada

Cynthia Liutkus-Pierce
Geologist
Location: the USA

In winter, Cynthia works in her university office in North Carolina. She gives lectures and she talks to her students every week. She often has meetings with other geologists. Every summer, she travels to Africa. She usually gets up and has breakfast at six o'clock in the morning because it's very hot. She never works late. She has dinner at eight o'clock. She goes to bed early, but she sometimes wakes up because the animals are noisy.

Julia Mayo Torne
Archaeologist
Location: Panama

Julia is originally from Panama. After twenty years in Spain, she's in Panama again. Her typical day changes with the seasons. In the dry season, Julia goes to her site. It's a good site and she usually finds objects every day. She often has lunch at the site. In the evening, she always has coffee with her colleagues. They talk about their day. Then she reads before she goes to bed. In the rainy season, Julia returns to her laboratory. She studies the objects from the site, and writes articles and reports.

Grammar **frequency adverbs**

4 Look at the grammar box. Then look at the article. <u>Underline</u> the frequency adverbs.

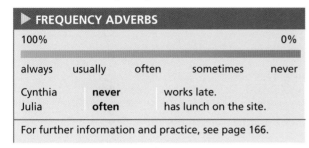

▶ FREQUENCY ADVERBS				
100%				0%
always	usually	often	sometimes	never
Cynthia	**never**	works late.		
Julia	**often**	has lunch on the site.		

For further information and practice, see page 166.

5 Rewrite the sentences with the adverb in the correct position.

1 Julia gets up early. (sometimes)
2 Julia has lunch with her colleagues. (always)
3 Cynthia goes to Africa in summer. (always)
4 Julia reads novels. (usually)
5 Cynthia travels in winter. (never)
6 Cynthia writes reports. (often)

6 Make the sentences in Exercise 5 true for you. Tell your partner.

Listening

7 🔊 **2.19** Listen to a conversation about Cynthia Liutkus-Pierce. Number the questions (1–6).

a Does she go to Africa every year?
b Does she work at this university?   *1*
c What does she do?
d Does she give lectures?
e Where does Cynthia go?
f Does she teach languages?

8 🔊 **2.19** Listen again. Write the answers to the questions.

Grammar **present simple questions** *he/she*

9 Look at the grammar box. Find the questions in Exercise 7.

▶ PRESENT SIMPLE QUESTIONS *HE/SHE*				
What Where	**does**	he/she	**do?** **work?**	He/She's a geologist. He/She **works** in Africa.
	Does	he/she	**work** at this university?	
	Yes, No,	he/she	**does.** **doesn't.**	

For further information and practice, see page 166.

10 Put the words in order to make questions.

1 Julia / does / where / work / ?
2 meet / does / who / Cynthia / ?
3 Cynthia / schoolchildren / teach / does / ?
4 Julia / like / does / coffee / ?
5 does / have lunch / where / Julia / ?
6 Cynthia / does / what time / get up / ?

11 Work in pairs. Ask and answer the questions. Use the information in the article.

Vocabulary **job activities**

12 Match a verb in A with words in B. Then <u>underline</u> four things that Cynthia does.

A	B
gives	articles / books
has	late / at home
talks	<u>lectures</u> / talks
travels	meetings / lunch
works	to different cities / countries / places
writes	to students / people / customers

13 Look at these jobs. Write sentences with the expressions in Exercise 12.

a journalist   a waiter   a businesswoman

a nurse   a receptionist   a shop assistant

Speaking

14 Work in pairs. Tell your partner about your friends and family. Use the words in Exercise 13.

> *My brother travels in his job. He's a businessman.*

15 Work in pairs. Ask your partner five questions about one of the people in Exercise 14.

> *Where does your brother travel to?*

> *He goes to different cities.*

> *Does he travel every week?*

> *No, he doesn't. He travels every month.*

8c Cats in crisis

Reading

1 Work in pairs. Match the animals in the photos (1–4) with the places (a–d).

a   Africa and Asia
b   Asia
c   South America
d   Africa

1 a jaguar

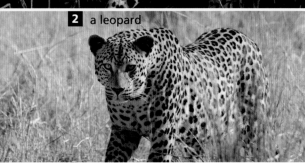

2 a leopard

3 a lion

4 a tiger

2 Work in pairs. Do you think the sentences are true (T) or false (F)?

1   Tigers are wild animals.
2   They eat animals.
3   They sleep at night.
4   They hunt people.
5   Thailand has a lot of tigers.
6   Tigers live in forests.

3 Read the article on page 99. Check your answers from Exercise 2.

4 Read the article again. Find these things.

1   one thing a tiger does at night
2   one thing Saksit Simcharoen does at night
3   two things Saksit Simcharoen does every month
4   one other thing he does in his job

5 Answer the questions.

1   How many wild tigers are in Asia today?
2   How many people work in the Huai Kha Khaeng Wildlife Park?
3   How does Saksit study the tigers in the park?
4   How many tigers in the park have radio collars?
5   How often does Saksit write a report?

Grammar *How ... ?*

6 Look at the grammar box. Choose the correct option.

We use 'how' *to ask for information / for a 'yes' or 'no' answer.*

> ▶ **HOW ... ?**
>
> **How** does Saksit study the tigers in the park?
> **How many** people does Saskit work with?
> **How often** does Saksit write a report?
>
> For further information and practice, see page 166.

7 Put the words in order to make questions with *how*. Then work in pairs. Ask and answer the questions with your partner.

1   tigers / how many / in the park / are / ?
2   in the park / cameras / are / how many / ?
3   have / how often / a meeting / Saksit / does / ?
4   help / we / can / tiger conservation / how / ?

8 Word focus *every*

a Look at the sentences. Which words can follow *every*?

1   Every month Saksit writes reports.
2   Does she go to Africa every year?
3   Does he travel every week?
4   Rosanna doesn't work every day.
5   I have a meeting every Tuesday.

b Write five sentences about you. Use the expressions with *every*. Read your sentences to your partner. What do you have in common?

Speaking

9 Tigers are night animals. What about you? Are you a 'morning person' or an 'evening person'? Do a quiz.

Student A: Turn to page 155.

Student B: Turn to page 159.

CATS IN CRISIS

'BIG CATS' IS THE NAME FOR TIGERS, LIONS, LEOPARDS
AND JAGUARS. THE 'BIG CATS' ARE IN CRISIS.

A tiger in the forest at night in Sumatra, Indonesia
Photo by Steve Winter

Tigers

number of wild tigers
in 1900 – 100,000
in 2010 – 3,500

Tigers live in many places in Asia – from very cold mountains in the Himalaya to very hot areas. They usually live in places without people, but people sometimes move into the tigers' areas. Tigers eat other animals. They hunt at night. In places without people, tigers also hunt in the day. They usually kill wild animals, but they sometimes kill domestic animals. Tigers are in crisis because people move into their areas and local people sometimes kill them.

Tiger conservation

tigers in Huai Kha Khaeng
Wildlife Park
in 1980 – 20
in 2010 – 60

Saksit Simcharoen works at the Huai Kha Khaeng Wildlife Park in Thailand. The park is a tiger conservation area. It's a very good place for tigers. About sixty tigers live there. Saksit works with 170 people in the park. He studies the park's tigers. Saksit goes into the forest at night. He doesn't see many tigers, but the park has 180 automatic cameras. They can take photos of tigers. Saksit checks the cameras. About eight of the tigers in the park have radio collars. Every month Saksit writes reports about the tigers in the area and he has a meeting with his colleagues. Saksit loves his job because the tigers in the park are not in crisis.

Saksit Simcharoen and his team
in Thailand measure and put a radio collar on a tiger.

automatic (adj) /ˌɔːtəˈmætɪk/ without a human
operator
conservation (n) /ˌkɒnsəˈveɪʃən/ protection
crisis (n) /ˈkraɪsɪs/ a difficult or dangerous time
domestic (adj) /dəˈmestɪk/ not wild, connected
with people and homes

a radio collar (n) /ˌreɪdɪəʊ ˈkɒlə/

8d One moment, please

Real life **on the phone**

1 🎧 **2.20** Listen to three phone calls (1–3). Who does the caller want to speak to? Write the number of the conversation. Can the people answer the call?

a   Mrs Jackson
b   Ed Carr
c   Mr Watts

2 🎧 **2.21** Look at the photos. Then listen to two of the phone calls again. Why doesn't the caller speak to the person? Tick (✓) the reasons.

3 Look at the expressions for ON THE PHONE. Write caller (C) or receptionist (R).

> ▶ **ON THE PHONE**
>
> Good morning, / Hello, PJ International.
> Can I help you?
> Yes, can I speak to Ed Carr, please?
> Yes, one moment, please.
> I'm sorry. He's/She's in a meeting.
> OK. Thank you. / Thanks.
> I'll call back later.

4 Complete the conversation with the expressions.

R: _____ , City College.
_____ ?
C: Yes, _____
Mrs Jackson, please?
R: _____ .
She's out of the office at the moment.
C: OK, thank you. _____
_____ .
Goodbye.
R: Goodbye.

5 Pronunciation **/s/ and /z/**

a 🎧 **2.22** Listen to these words. Is the <u>s</u> like *this* or *is*?

> | | | | |
> |---|---|---|---|
> | plea<u>s</u>e | he'<u>s</u> | ye<u>s</u> | Friday<u>s</u> |
> | work<u>s</u> | thank<u>s</u> | | |

b 🎧 **2.22** Listen again and repeat the words.

6 Work in pairs. Practise phone calls. Use the ideas in the photos.

works from home on Fridays

out of the office

on holiday

with a customer

doesn't work in the afternoons

in a meeting

8e My new job

Writing an email

1 Read Vijay's email about his new job in a call centre. Complete the email with seven of these words.

> classmates   colleagues   evening   job   morning
> office   phone calls   tasks   work

2 Read the email again. Who do you think the email is to?

a   his boss
b   his friend
c   his colleague

> Hi!
>
> Here I am in my new ¹ _____ ! It's good!
> I ² _____ from Monday to Friday. The
> ³ _____ opens at 8.00 a.m. I usually arrive at
> about 7.45 and I have coffee with my ⁴ _____ .
> They're great. We have a meeting every ⁵ _____
> and the boss gives us our ⁶ _____ for the day.
> I usually make about 40 ⁷ _____ every day. I
> finish early on Fridays – let's meet for lunch. How
> about next week?
>
> Vijay

3 Writing skill spelling: double letters

a Look at the email again. <u>Underline</u> the words with double letters.

b Complete the words with the letter. How many words have double letters?

1 ar_____ist (t)   6   di_____icult (f)
2 busine_____man (s)   7   di_____er (n)
3 cla_____es (s)   8   m_____t (e)
4 co_____ege (l)   9   su_____er (m)
5 di_____erent (f)   10 w_____kend (e)

c Complete the email from a student with words from Exercises 1 and 3b.

> Hi!
>
> Here I am at my new ¹ _____ ! It's good! I have
> ² _____ every day except Wednesday. My
> courses aren't ³ _____ . I usually do about two
> essays every week. I often go out with my
> ⁴ _____ in the evenings. They're great. Let's
> ⁵ _____ and play tennis one day. How about
> next ⁶ _____ ?
>
> Jim

4 Write an email to a friend about your new job or your new course. Include a suggestion to meet.

5 Check your email. Check the spelling.

6 Work in pairs. Exchange emails. Reply to your partner's email.

The elephants of Samburu

An elephant at night in Samburu National Reserve

Before you watch

1 Work in pairs. Look at the photo and the caption. Where does this elephant live?

2 🔊 **2.23** Look at the word box. Listen and repeat the words.

3 Read about Samburu. Answer the questions.

1 Where is the Samburu National Reserve?
2 What does the organisation *Save the Elephants* do?
3 How does *Google Earth* help *Save the Elephants*?

> The Samburu National Reserve is in Kenya. Lions, leopards, elephants and buffalo live in the reserve. The reserve is the home of the conservation organisation *Save the Elephants*.
> *Save the Elephants* works in elephant conservation in four places in Africa: Kenya, Mali, Gabon and South Africa. *Save the Elephants* works with *Google Earth*. *Google Earth* can follow elephants with GPS collars.

While you watch

4 Work in pairs. How much do you know about elephants? Choose the option you think is correct.

1 Elephants live *in family groups / alone*.
2 Elephants *like / don't like* water.
3 Elephants eat *plants / animals*.
4 Elephants *hunt / sleep* at night.

5 Watch the video. Check your answers from Exercise 4.

6 Read the sentences. Watch the video again. Choose the correct option (a–c).

1 Nick Nichols
   a is a photographer for *National Geographic*.
   b is a student.
   c works for *Save the Elephants*.

2 Daniel Lentipo
   a is a photographer for *National Geographic*.
   b is a student.
   c works for *Save the Elephants*.

3 Daniel teaches Nick how to
   a take photos of the elephants.
   b identify individual elephants.
   c follow elephants.

4 Nick and Daniel follow the elephants for
   a four hours every day.
   b eight hours every day.
   c ten hours every day.

5 Elephants put their trunks up
   a at night.
   b to greet other elephants.
   c when they are thirsty.

7 Watch the video again. Write three things:
   1 the elephants do every day.
   2 Nick and Daniel do every day.

After you watch

8 Read about Nick and Daniel's work routine. Complete the text with the correct form of these verbs.

drive	get up	start	study	take
work	work			

Nick Nichols [1] _____ for *National Geographic*. Daniel Lentipo is the Chief Research Assistant at the Samburu National Reserve. Nick and Daniel [2] _____ early every day. They [3] _____ work early. Daniel [4] _____ the jeep and he [5] _____ the elephants. Nick [6] _____ photos of the elephants. Nick and Daniel sometimes [7] _____ at night. Nick's photos of sleeping elephants are very unusual.

9 Work in pairs.

Student A: You are a photographer.

Student B. You are a journalist.

Prepare answers to these questions. Then take turns to ask and answer the questions.

- Who do you work for?
- Where do you work?
- Where do you travel to in your job?
- What do you take photos of / write about?
- What's a typical day like in your job?

call (v) /kɔːl/ to make a noise (animal or bird)	**identify** (v) /aɪˈdentɪfaɪ/ to find
follow (v) /ˈfɒləʊ/ to travel behind a person or animal	an **individual** (n) /ɪndɪˈvɪdjuəl/ one person or animal
gentle (adj) /ˈdʒentəl/ kind	a **jeep** (n) /dʒiːp/
greet (v) /griːt/ to say 'hello'	**lie down** (v) /ˌlaɪ ˈdaʊn/
a **hand** (n) /hænd/	**sleep** (v) /sliːp/
have a bath (v) /hæv ə bɑːθ/	a **trunk** (n) /trʌŋk/

UNIT 8 REVIEW

Grammar

1 Read about Joel Murray. Write eight sentences with the <u>underlined</u> words. Use *he*.

Hi. I'm Joel. I'm 46. I'm a truck driver. ¹I have a new <u>job</u>. In my new job, ²I drive <u>from New Mexico to Arizona</u> every week. That's about 2,400 kilometres. ³I work <u>Monday to Friday</u>. ⁴I start work early – at <u>six o'clock</u>. ⁵I don't have <u>breakfast</u>, but ⁶I eat <u>a snack</u> in my truck. ⁷I have lunch in <u>a snack bar</u> with other drivers. ⁸I work <u>late</u>.

2 Rewrite sentences 3, 6 and 8 with these adverbs:

   3 usually   6 sometimes   8 often

3 Complete the sentences with prepositions.

1 Joel drives to Arizona _____ Mondays and Wednesdays.
2 He doesn't work _____ the evening.
3 He finishes work _____ 4.30 in the afternoon.
4 He has a holiday _____ August.

4 Complete the questions with three of these expressions. Then answer the questions.

How	How many	How much	How often
How old			

1 _____ is Joel?
2 _____ kilometres does he drive every week?
3 _____ does Joel work late?

I CAN
say what people do every day (present simple)
say when people do things (prepositions of time)
say how often people do things (frequency adverbs)
use *how* correctly

Vocabulary

5 Match a verb from A with a word from B.

A	B
finish	breakfast
get up	dinner
go	early
have	lunch
have	to bed
have	work
start	work

6 Work in pairs. Ask and answer questions about your day with the expressions from Exercise 5.

7 Complete the sentences with these verbs. You can use some verbs more than once.

talk	travel	work	write

1 Journalists _____ articles.
2 Nurses _____ to people.
3 Businessmen _____ to different countries.
4 Shop assistants _____ to customers.
5 Waiters _____ late.
6 Artists _____ at home.

I CAN
talk about routines
talk about job activities

Real life

8 Put the phone conversation between a businessman and a receptionist in order.

a Hello.
b Oh. Well, can I speak to her assistant?
c Yes, can I speak to Ms Becker, please?
d Can I help you?
e I'm sorry. She's on holiday this week.
f Good morning, Sports Unlimited.   *1*
g OK. Thank you.
h Yes, one moment please.

I CAN
say why people can't answer a phone call
make phone calls

Speaking

9 Work in pairs. Take turns.

Student A: You have a new job as a driver.

Student B: Ask your friend about his/her new job. Use the ideas below.

what / do?	what time / start?
where / work?	how often / work late?
how many days / work?	you / like the job?

10 Ask and answer the questions.

A passenger shows her passport and train ticket at Machu Picchu village train station, Peru.
Photo by Michael S. Lewis

FEATURES

1 Work in pairs. Look at the photo. Who does the woman work for (a–c)? Who are the other people?

a a bus company   b a rail company   c an airline

2 2.24 Listen to four people talk about travel. Write the number of the speaker (1–4) next to the picture.

by boat   by bus   by plane   by train

3 2.24 Listen again. Do all the people travel? Complete the table.

	Where?	When?
1		*every week*
2		
3		
4		

4 Work in pairs. Ask and answer questions about travel with *where, when* and *how*?

Where do you travel to?

I travel to Moscow and Kiev.

9a Travel essentials

Vocabulary clothes

1 🔘 **2.25** Look at the photos. Listen and repeat the words.

a pair of boots

a hat

a pair of sandals

a T-shirt

a coat

a jacket

a skirt

a pair of jeans

a top

a dress

a pair of shoes

a shirt

a pair of trousers

a scarf

a pair of shorts

a jumper

2 Work in pairs. Look at the people in your class. Match clothes with names.

> *A white shirt and a pair of black trousers.*

> *Ramon?*

> *Yes.*

3 Work in pairs. Talk about your clothes.

What do you usually wear … ?
- for work
- at college
- at the weekend
- on holiday

> *I usually wear a dress for work.*

Reading

4 Read the article by Kate Renshaw. <u>Underline</u> the clothes.

5 Read the article again. What does Kate always take with her? What about her sister and her husband?

6 What do you never travel without? Tell your partner.

By Kate Renshaw

TRAVEL *essentials*

I'm a travel writer. I usually travel alone, but my family sometimes comes with me. It's difficult because they always have a lot of bags – look at this photo of our trip to Ecuador! There are eight people and there are about fifteen bags! In my sister's bags there are three jackets, four or five jumpers, seven pairs of trousers and two dresses. There are six or seven books too. She never travels without books. In my husband's bag there's a pair of boots, a pair of shoes and a pair of sandals! And his maps – he loves maps and he always takes maps on trips.

But when I travel alone, I take a very small suitcase. There's a pocket for my travel documents and inside there are two parts – one for clothes and one for my laptop. I never travel without my laptop! That's it!

Grammar *there is/are*

7 Look at the grammar box. Then look at the article. <u>Underline</u> the sentences with *there's* and *there are*.

▶ THERE IS/ARE			
There's	a	laptop	in my suitcase.
There are	two some	parts clothes	
(there's = there is)			

For further information and practice, see page 166.

8 🌀 **2.26** Make sentences about things in Kate's bags in the photo. Then listen and check.

	a camera.
	a laptop.
	three scarves.
There's	two shirts.
There are	a pair of shoes.
	a skirt.
	some T-shirts.

9 Pronunciation *there are*

🌀 **2.27** Listen and repeat the sentences with *there are* from Exercise 8. Is the word *are* stressed?

Speaking and writing

10 How many countries can you name? Imagine you travel a lot. Choose three countries to complete the sentences. Write a list of the things you pack in your suitcase for each trip.

1 I travel to _____ for my job.
2 I go to _____ for my holiday.
3 I go to _____ to visit my family.

11 Work in pairs. Tell your partner where you go and what's in your suitcase.

> *I often travel to Singapore for my job. In my suitcase today, there's a pair of shoes …*

9b Places to stay

Listening

There are cheap rooms at this youth hostel in Cape Town.

The expensive, but very comfortable, Southern Sun The Cullinan Hotel in Cape Town.

1 Look at the photos. Which people stay in these two places when they travel?

> business travellers   families
> students   young couples

2 🎧 **2.28** Listen to Sandra and Luke plan their trip to Cape Town. Read Luke's questions and underline the words he uses.

1 Are there any hotels near the *airport / beach*?
2 Is there a youth hostel *in the city centre / near the airport*?
3 Is there *a bus / a train* to the city centre?

3 🎧 **2.28** Listen again. Are the sentences true (T) or false (F)?

1 There's a youth hostel near the airport.
2 There are some cheap hotels near the airport.
3 There's a train to the centre.

Grammar *there is/are* negative and question forms

4 Look at the sentences and questions in the grammar box. When do we use *any*?

▶ *THERE IS /ARE* NEGATIVE AND QUESTION FORMS		
There **isn't**	a train.	
There **aren't**	**any** cheap hotels.	
Is there	a youth hostel?	Yes, there **is**. No, there **isn't**.
Are there	**any** hotels?	Yes, there **are**. No, there **aren't**.
For further information and practice, see page 166.		

5 Work in pairs. Tell your partner the name of your hometown or a place you know. Write questions about your partner's town. Use *Is there a/an ... ? / Are there any ... ?*

airport nice beach cheap restaurants expensive hotels good hotels tourist attractions youth hostels	in near	the city/town the centre

6 Work in pairs. Ask and answer your questions from Exercise 5.

> *Are there any good hotels near the centre?*

> *Yes, there are. There are five or six four-star hotels.*

7 Write true sentences with the information from Exercise 6. Use affirmative and negative forms.

Vocabulary **furniture**

8 🔊 **2.29** Look at the photos (1–12). Then listen and repeat the words. Write the words with the photos.

armchair	bath	bed	chair	desk	fridge
lamp	shower	sofa	table	TV	wardrobe

1 ....

2 ....

3 ....

4 ....

5 ....

6 ....

7 ....

8 ....

9 ....

10 ....

11 ....

12 ....

9 Work in pairs. Which things are there usually in a hotel room?

> *There's a bed, …*

10 🔊 **2.30** Sandra and Luke are in their hotel room in Cape Town. Listen to their conversation. Tick (✓) the things in Exercise 8 they talk about.

11 🔊 **2.30** Listen again. Choose the correct room (a or b).

a

b

Speaking

12 Work in pairs. You are in a hotel. Ask and answer questions about your hotel bedroom.

Student A: Turn to page 156.

Student B: Turn to page 160.

9c Across a continent

Reading

1 Work in pairs. Look at the map and the photos on page 111. What things do you think you can see or do on a trip across Russia?

2 Read the article on page 111 and check your ideas from Exercise 1. Then find the places in the article on the map.

3 Read the article again. Are the sentences true (T) or false (F)?

1 There's a road from Moscow to Vladivostok.
2 There are two trains every day from Moscow to Vladivostok.
3 You can't sleep on the train.
4 You can leave the train and stay in hotels.
5 There aren't any towns near Lake Baikal.
6 The Trans-Siberian Highway is only for lorries.

4 Work in pairs. Is this the kind of holiday you like? What do you like?

> *I love trips to different countries.*

> *I like beach holidays.*

Vocabulary travel

5 Match a verb in A with words in B. Check your answers in the article.

A	B
travel	a bus
leave	an ice cave
book	from east to west
use	home
stay	in hotels
visit	in Vladivostock
take	Moscow
drive	your tickets
arrive	a travel agent
fly	your car

6 Complete the sentences with verbs from Exercise 5.

1 'What time does your plane .... in Moscow?'
   'At 8.40 in the morning.'
2 We don't .... in expensive hotels.
3 I usually .... my tickets with a travel agent.
4 A boat .... Vladivostok for Japan every week.
5 Let's .... a bus from the airport.
6 'Is there an airport in Irkutsk? Can you .... there?'
   'Yes, there is.'

7 Word focus *take*

a Look at these expressions with *take*. Find one of the expressions in the article on page 111.

> take a bus   take a photo   take a suitcase

b Work in pairs. Ask and answer the questions.

1 How many suitcases do you take when you travel?
2 Do you usually take photos when you are on holiday?
3 Do you often take a taxi / a bus / a train / a plane? Where to?

Grammar imperative forms

8 Look at the sentences from the article in the grammar box. Are the words in **bold** nouns or verbs?

> ▶ **IMPERATIVE FORMS**
>
> **Book** your tickets in advance.
> **Don't wait** until you arrive.
>
> (don't = do not)
>
> For further information and practice, see page 167.

9 Complete these sentences from the article with the missing verb.

1 .... non-stop in seven days.
2 .... in hotels.
3 .... sightseeing in the big cities.
4 .... on a day trip.
5 .... the new Trans-Siberian Highway.
6 .... your car.

Writing and speaking

10 Work in pairs. Write five tips for travellers in your country or a country you know. Think of reasons for the tips.

Don't travel by bus.

11 Work in groups of four. Discuss your travel tips. Ask follow-up questions.

> *Don't travel by bus.*
> *Why?*
> *The buses are very slow.*

Across a continent *by rail* and *by road*

Russia is a very large country. There are eight time zones between Moscow in the west and Vladivostok in the east. It's 9,000 kilometres and there are two ways to travel – by rail and by road.

BY RAIL: THE TRANS-SIBERIAN RAILWAY

Trains leave Moscow almost every day. Book your tickets in advance – don't wait until you arrive in Moscow. You can book online or use a travel agent. There are two options:

Travel non-stop in seven days. You sleep and eat on the train. You can talk to other passengers, learn some words in Russian and enjoy the views. The train travels through amazing mountains, beautiful forests and strange deserts.

Stop on the way and stay in hotels. Go sightseeing in the big cities. In Novosibirsk – the main city in Siberia – there are museums, art galleries, theatres and a famous opera house in the city centre. Or visit the Kungur Ice Cave near Perm. From the towns of Irkutsk or Ulan-Ude, you can take a bus or train to Lake Baikal, a UNESCO World Heritage site. Lake Baikal is 636 kilometres long and there are only four or five towns near it. The lake is a great place for sports activities – diving, hiking and horse riding are all popular.

BY ROAD: THE TRANS-SIBERIAN HIGHWAY

Are you adventurous? Then take the new Trans-Siberian Highway. Drive your car or – for the trip of a lifetime – hitch-hike with Russian drivers in their cars and lorries.

And when you finally arrive in Vladivostock, you can fly home or continue your trip – there's a boat to Japan every week.

adventurous (adj) /ədˈventʃərəs/ an *adventurous* person likes danger
(do it) **in advance** (exp) /ɪn ədˈvɑːns/ to do one thing before another thing
hitch-hike (v) /hɪtʃhaɪk/ to travel for free
lifetime (n) /ˈlaɪftaɪm/ all of your life

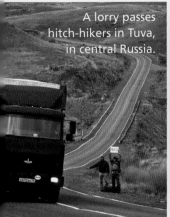

A lorry passes hitch-hikers in Tuva, in central Russia.

9d At the hotel

Vocabulary **hotel services**

1 Match the hotel services (1–5) in the brochure with the explanations (a–e).

Guest services – numbers

1	room service	101
2	alarm call	110
3	business centre	109
	(open 06.00–12.00)	
4	laundry	111
5	medical service	112

THE MARLIN HOTEL

a a doctor or nurse
b meals in your hotel room
c a service to wash or clean your clothes
d a room with computers, printers and Internet
e a telephone call to wake up in the morning

2 Which services do you think business travellers use? And tourists?

Real life **requests**

3 Read part of a conversation between a hotel guest and a receptionist. Match the requests (1–4) with the responses (a–d).

1 I'd like an alarm call at 7.30, please.
2 I'd like to have a meal in my room this evening.
3 I'd like to use the Internet.
4 Is there a bank near the hotel?

a Yes, there's one in this street.
b In the morning? Certainly, sir.
c No problem, sir. There's wi-fi in all the rooms.
d Of course. There's a menu in your room.

4 🎵 **2.31** Listen and check your answers from Exercise 3.

5 🎵 **2.31** Listen again and answer the questions.

1 What's the guest's room number?
2 Where's the menu?
3 Where's the bank?

▶ **REQUESTS**

I'd like an alarm call at 7.30, please.
I'd like to have a meal in my room.
I'd like to book a taxi.
Certainly, sir/madam.
Of course.
That's no problem.

6 Pronunciation **I'd like**

a 🎵 **2.32** Listen and repeat three sentences from the conversation.

b Work in pairs. Practise these requests. Use *I'd like a …* or *I'd like to …* .

breakfast in my room	use the Internet
an alarm call	see a doctor

I'd like breakfast in my room.   *That's no problem.*

7 Work in pairs. Look at the audioscript on page 173. Practise the conversation.

8 Work in pairs.

Student A: You are a hotel guest. Make two requests and/or ask for information.

Student B: You are the hotel receptionist. Respond to the requests and/or answer the questions.

Take turns. Use the ideas in Exercise 6b and those below.

room service
book a table in the restaurant
use the business centre
stay an extra night
make an international phone call
a bus stop near the hotel?
metro station near the hotel?

9e A great place for a weekend

Writing **travel advice**

1 Read the advice on a travel website. Answer the questions.

1 What's the name of the city?
2 How can you travel there?
3 Where can you eat?
4 What can you eat?
5 What can you see?
6 What can you do?

2 Read the advice again. <u>Underline</u> four tips from Dani.

3 Writing skill *because*

a Look at the sentence from the text. Find two more sentences with *because*.

Lisbon is a great place for a weekend **because** *there is a lot to see and do.*

b Rewrite these sentences with *because*.

1 Go in spring. It's very hot in summer.
2 Travel by bus. It's cheap.
3 Book your hotel in advance. It's a very popular place.
4 You can take a boat trip. It's on a river.

4 Make notes about a place you know. Use the questions in Exercise 1.

5 Use your notes and write two or three paragraphs of advice for travellers to the place. Include at least one tip.

6 Check your advice. Check the spelling, the punctuation and the verbs.

7 Work in pairs. Exchange advice. Is your partner's place a good place to travel to?

POPULAR PLACES IN EUROPE: **LISBON**

◀ YOUR PHOTOS

YOUR TRAVEL ADVICE ▼

Dani, London.

Date of trip: 22–24 June

Lisbon is a great place for a weekend because there is a lot to see and do! There are flights from the main European cities every day. There's a bus from the airport to the city. Or take a taxi because they aren't expensive. Travel around the city by tram – they're great!

There are great cafés and restaurants in every street. And try the delicious Portuguese cakes!

There are some beautiful buildings in Lisbon. And don't miss a Fado show because this Portuguese music is very beautiful.

9f Along the Inca Road

A woman walks along an ancient Inca road.

Before you watch

1 Look at the photo and the caption. The Inca road system goes through Ecuador, Peru, Bolivia, Chile and Argentina. How old is it? Choose the correct option (a–c).

a 50 years old
b 500 years old
c 5,000 years old

2 💿 **2.33** Look at the word box. Listen and repeat the words.

3 Work in pairs. Read the introduction to the video. What things do you think you can see or do on a trip along the Inca Road?

Along the Inca Road
Part 1 – from goldmines to landmines

Karin Muller is an American adventurer and writer. She is on a trip through South America to explore the cultures and people along the Inca Road. She travels more than 3,000 miles through four countries. Her adventure begins in Ecuador.

While you watch

4 Watch the video without sound. Tick (✓) the things you see.

a plane	a lorry
a donkey	a bus
a camel	a sheep
a helicopter	a horse
a bicycle	a llama
a canoe	a train

5 Read the questions. Watch and listen to the video. Choose the correct option or options (a–c).

1 Where does Karin start her trip?
  a in the United States
  b in Peru
  c in Ecuador

2 What can you buy at the village market?
  a animals   b snacks   c vegetables

3 Where does Karin walk on day 1?
  a across a desert
  b along a beach
  c through mountains

4 How does Karin travel?
  a hitch-hiking   b by train   c on foot

5 Who does Karin meet?
  a farmers   b passengers   c tourists

6 Watch the video again. Test your observation skills. Are these sentences true (T) or false (F)?

1 There's a young boy at the market.
2 There are three fish on Karin's plate.
3 The tent is orange and blue.
4 There's a woman on the road when Karin hitch-hikes.
5 There's a man in a blue shirt at the bus stop.
6 On the beach, Karin wears a hat.

After you watch

7 Match the two parts of the sentences about Karin.

1 She goes canoeing   a a lot of people.
2 She hitch-hikes   b across sand dunes.
3 She rides   c in a river.
4 She walks   d in the back of a lorry.
5 She meets   e on a road.

8 Work in pairs. Have two conversations:

1 At the market food stall

Student A: You are Karin. Ask about the food and buy a snack.

Student B: You are the stall holder.

What's this?   *It's fish.*

2 Meeting people on a trip

Student A: You are the helicopter pilot.

Student B: You are Karin.

Hi. I'm .... . Nice to meet you.   *Hello. ...*

ancient (adj) /ˈeɪnʃənt/ very very old

a bang (n) /bæŋ/ very loud noise

a canoe (n) /kəˈnuː/

crash (v) /kræʃ/

a donkey (n) /ˈdɒŋki/

gold (n) /gəʊld/ a metal in jewellery

a goldmine (n) /ˈgəʊldmaɪn/ a place to find gold

a landmine (n) /ˈlændmaɪn/ a type of bomb

a llama (n) /ˈlɑːmə/

loud (adj) /laʊd/ very noisy

a plate (n) /pleɪt/

a sand dune (n) /ˈsænd ˌdjuːn/

a sheep (n) /ʃiːp/

a track (n) /træk/

UNIT 9 REVIEW

Grammar

1 Look at the photo. Write questions with *is there /*
are there?

1 _____ a map?
2 _____ a passport?
3 _____ books?
4 _____ hat?
5 _____ a camera?
6 _____ tickets?

2 Work in pairs. Ask and answer the questions in
Exercise 1. Take turns.

3 Are these sentences true (T) or false (F)? Change
the false sentences so they are true.

1 There isn't a map.
2 There's a passport.
3 There are some books.
4 There are two pens.
5 There isn't a pair of boots.
6 There aren't any tickets.

4 Put the words in order.

1 late / be / don't
2 moment / a / wait
3 night / travel / don't / at
4 winter / in / go
5 cafés / try / local / the
6 stay / hotel / this / don't / in

I CAN	
use *there is* and *there are* correctly	☐
give instructions (imperative forms)	☐

Vocabulary

5 Read the sentences. Which options are not logical?

1 In cold weather, I wear *a pair of sandals / a coat /*
a pair of boots / a hat.
2 In hot weather, I wear *a T-shirt / a pair of sandals /*
a skirt / a jacket.
3 At home, I wear *a jumper / a scarf / a pair of jeans /*
a top.
4 In the office, I wear *a pair of trousers / a T-shirt /*
a shirt / a pair of shoes.

6 Match the two parts to make sentences about a
hotel room.

1 There's a tourist   a is very small.
   information brochure   b on the table.
2 Is there one bed   c or two?
3 You can put these   d in the
   bottles   bathroom?
4 There's an armchair,   e in the fridge.
5 Is there a shower   f but there isn't a
6 The wardrobe   sofa.

7 Complete the sentences with six of these verbs.

arrives	book	drives	leaves	stay	take
travels	visit				

1 We usually _____ our tickets online.
2 The train _____ in Oslo at midnight.
3 We can _____ a bus to the airport.
4 Our plane _____ Oslo at 10.20.
5 We often _____ in cheap hotels.
6 We usually _____ the museums.

I CAN	
talk about clothes	☐
talk about furniture	☐
talk about travel	☐
talk about hotel services	☐

Real life

8 Complete the requests (1–4) in a hotel. Then match
the requests with the responses (a–d).

breakfast	room service	stay	use

1 I'd like to _____ the Internet.
2 I'd like _____ at 7.30 a.m., please.
3 I'd like to _____ an extra night.
4 I'd like _____ .

a That's no problem. The restaurant is open from
   7.00 a.m.
b Of course. The number is 101.
c Certainly, sir. What's your name?
d That's no problem. There's wi-fi in your room.

I CAN	
make and respond to requests	☐
ask for and give information	☐

Speaking

9 Work in groups. You work in the tourist
information centre of the town you are in (or town
you all know). What is there for visitors to do and
to see in the area? List at least six things and say
where the places are.

Unit 10 History

Photo by Willard Culver

FEATURES

1 🔊 **2.34** Work in pairs. Look at the photo and discuss the questions. Then listen and check your answers.

  1 Where do you think the men are?
    a at home   b in a television studio
    c in a laboratory
  2 What year do you think it is?
    a 1926   b 1950   c 1973
  3 What invention does the photo show?
    a video recorders   b colour television
    c digital television

2 🔊 **2.35** Listen and repeat the years. Then match the inventions with the years.

Year	Invention
1950	Blu-ray discs
1963	colour television
1973	digital cameras
1975	digital television
1993	mobile phones
1995	MP3 players
2006	video recorders

3 🔊 **2.36** Listen and check your answers from Exercise 2.

4 Work in pairs. Choose and write five years in a list. Dictate these years to your partner. Then compare your lists.

10a Explorers

The first American expedition on Everest in 1963
Photo by National Geographic expedition photographer and writer Barry Bishop

Reading and listening

1 Look at the photo of two mountaineers. Where are they? Read the caption and check your answer.

2 🔊 **2.37** Read the quiz. Complete the sentences with the names. Then listen and check.

captain (n) /ˈkæptɪn/ a leader or commander
expedition (n) /ˌekspəˈdɪʃən/ a trip with scientists and/or explorers

North Pole (n) /ˌnɔːθ ˈpəʊl/
South Pole (n) /ˌsaʊθ ˈpəʊl/
round the world (exp)
 /raʊnd ðə wɜːld/
space (n) /speɪs/

North Pole
space
round the world
South Pole

Ferdinand Magellan

Yuri Gagarin

Roald Amundsen

Junko Tabei

Ann Bancroft

Valentina Tereshkova

Explorers Quiz: historical moments

Do you know these famous explorers? Can you complete the 'firsts' with their names?

- The first round-the-world expedition was from 1519 to 1522. The expedition captain was ....

- The first successful South Pole expedition was in 1911. The expedition leader was ....

- The first man in space was .... The first woman in space was .... They were both from Russia.

- On 16 May 1975, ... was the first woman at the top of Everest.

- The first woman at the North Pole was .... on 1 May 1986.

3 **2.38** Read and listen to the texts (1–4). Match the texts with four of the people from the quiz.

1 She was born in 1939. She was in a team of Japanese mountaineers. They were all women.

2 He was born in 1480. He was Portuguese, but he was an explorer for the Spanish king Carlos I.

3 She was born in the United States on 29 September 1955. She was the leader of an expedition to the South Pole in 1993. All the people on the expedition were women.

4 He was from Norway and he was born on 16 July 1872. His parents were rich. His father was a sea captain.

Grammar *was/were*

4 Look at the past forms of *be* in the grammar box. Underline these forms in the texts in Exercise 3.

▶ *WAS/WERE*		
I/He/She/It	**was**	born in 1480. an explorer. Portuguese.
You/We/You/They	**were**	explorers. from Russia.
For further information and practice, see page 167.		

5 **Pronunciation** *was/were* weak forms

a **2.39** Listen and repeat five sentences from the grammar box.

b Complete the sentences for you. Read them to your partner. What do you have in common?

1 I _____ born in _____ [place].
2 My parents _____ born in _____ [place] (and _____ [place]).
3 My father _____ born in _____ [year].
4 My mother _____ born in _____ [year].

6 Complete the paragraphs with *was* and *were*.

Yuri Gagarin ¹ _____ born in 1934. His parents ² _____ farmers. From 1955 to 1961, he ³ _____ a pilot. The first space rockets ⁴ _____ small and so the first people in space ⁵ _____ small too. Gagarin ⁶ _____ a small man – 1.57 metres.

Valentina Tereshkova ⁷ _____ born in 1937 in central Russia. Her parents ⁸ _____ from Belarus. She ⁹ _____ a factory worker. After their trips into space, on 12 April 1961 and 16 June 1963, Gagarin and Tereshkova ¹⁰ _____ famous all over the world.

Vocabulary dates

7 Look at *Important dates in exploration*. Complete the dates with information from the quiz.

Important dates in exploration	
1st _____	first woman at the North Pole
2nd June 1953	news of first men on Everest
3rd November 1957	Sputnik II into space
4th October 1957	Sputnik I into space
5th / 6th / 7th / 8th / 9th / 10th / 11th	
12th April 1961	first man in space
13th December 1972	last man on the moon
14th December 1911	first people at the South Pole
15th	
16th _____	first woman at the top of Everest
17th / 18th / 19th	
20th July 1969	first men on the moon

8 **2.40** Look at *Important dates in exploration*. Listen and repeat the ordinal numbers.

9 **2.41** Say these ordinal numbers. Then listen and check.

21st	22nd	23rd	24th	25th	26th
27th	28th	29th	30th	31st	

10 **2.42** Look at the example. Then listen and repeat the dates.

Example:
the first of May 1986

Speaking

11 Work in pairs. What are three important dates in your country?

The 14th of July is Bastille Day.

12 Work in pairs.

Student A: Dictate five important dates from your past to your partner.

Student B: Say the dates.

Student A: Say why the date was important.

the first of September 1990

It was my first day at school.

10b Heroes

Reading and listening

1 Work in pairs. Look at the photos of the
people. What do you know about them?

> *Who's this?*

> *I'm not sure. I think
> he's a sportsman.*

2 Read the information about the radio programme
Heroes. Answer the questions.

1 When is the programme on the radio?
2 What do the people on the programme talk about?
3 Who is on the programme today?
4 Who were their heroes?

David Attenborough

Radio 6 19.30 13–18 March

Peter and Rose Harvey

Michael Johnson

Heroes

**Who was your hero when you
were young?**

In this programme, we talk to people
about their heroes. Today we hear about
Aneta's hero, the Olympic champion
Michael Johnson. Joe's hero wasn't happy
in his first job, but is now a very famous
television star – David Attenborough.
We also talk to Clare. Her heroes weren't
famous, but they were important to her.
They were her teachers at college.

3 🔊 **2.43** What do you think the people say about their heroes? Complete the sentences with these words. Then listen to the programme and check.

> animals   art   eight   first   friendly   funny
> great   interesting

1 He was a _____ sportsman.
2 He was the world champion _____ times.
3 His programmes about _____ and nature were fantastic.
4 His _____ job was with books.
5 All his programmes were really _____ .
6 The teachers were really nice and _____ .
7 Mrs Harvey was my _____ teacher.
8 She was very _____ .

4 🔊 **2.43** Listen again. Choose the correct answer to the interviewer's questions.

1 Was he the Olympic champion?
   Yes, he was. / No, he wasn't.
2 Were you good at sports at school?
   Yes, I was. / No, I wasn't.
3 Was it his first job?
   Yes, it was. / No, it wasn't.
4 Were you born then?
   Yes, I was. / No, I wasn't.
5 Were they good teachers?
   Yes, they were. / No, they weren't.

5 What can you remember? Write Aneta, Joe or Clare.

1 _____ wasn't happy at school.
2 _____ was in the basketball team at school.
3 _____ 's favourite programme was *Life on Earth*.

Grammar *was/were* negative and question forms

6 Look at the grammar box. How do we make the negative and question forms of *was* and *were*?

▶ *WAS/WERE* NEGATIVE AND QUESTION FORMS		
I/He/She/It	**wasn't**	happy.
We/You/They	**weren't**	famous.
Was	I/he/she/it	happy?	Yes, I/he/she/it **was**.
		famous?	No, I/he/she/it **wasn't**.
Were	you/we/they		Yes, you/we/you/they **were**.
			No, you/we/you/they **weren't**.
For further information and practice, see page 167.		

7 Pronunciation strong forms

a 🔊 **2.44** Listen and repeat these questions and answers from the radio programme.

1 <u>Was</u> he the Olympic champion?
   Yes, he <u>was</u>.
2 <u>Was</u> it his first job?
   No, it <u>wasn't</u>.
3 <u>Were</u> they good teachers?
   Yes, they <u>were</u>.

b 🔊 **2.44** Listen again. Are the <u>underlined</u> words weak or strong?

8 Write questions with *was* or *were*.

1 Michael Johnson / on TV / ?
2 your hero / David Attenborough / ?
3 your parents / famous / ?
4 you / happy at school / ?
5 your teachers / friendly / ?
6 you / good at sport / ?

9 Work in pairs. Think about when you were young. Ask and answer the questions in Exercise 8.

Vocabulary describing people

10 Work in pairs. Look at these words. Think of a person you both know for each word.

> famous   fantastic   friendly
> good   great   happy
> interesting   nice

Speaking

11 Write the names of two heroes from your past. Write the answers to these questions.

- Who was he/she?
- Was he/she on television? … famous? a teacher? a … ?
- Why was he/she your hero?

12 Work in groups. Write the names from Exercise 11 on pieces of paper. Mix them. Take turns to read a name. Ask and answer the questions about the names.

> *Who was Jill Roberts?*

> *She was my first boss.*

10c The first Americans

Reading

1 Work in pairs. Do you think these sentences are true (T) or false (F)?

1 The Inca Empire was in North America.
2 The Maya people were from Central America.
3 The Aztecs were from Peru.
4 The Sioux people were from South America.

2 Read the first paragraph of the article. Check your answers from Exercise 1.

3 Now read the rest of the article on page 123. Answer the questions.

1 Who was Tupac Amaru?
2 Who was Moctezuma?
3 Where were the Apache people from?
4 When was Geronimo born?
5 Why was Geronimo famous?

4 Who were important leaders in your country's history?

Vocabulary **time expressions**

5 <u>Underline</u> these words and expressions in the article. Do we use the words and expressions with verbs in the present or past form?

today	ago	at that time	now

6 Complete the sentences with words and expressions from Exercise 5. In two sentences more than one word is possible.

1 About two hundred years _____ Geronimo was born.
2 _____ people know the name 'Geronimo'.
3 _____ the Maya people live in Mexico.
4 _____ , the Native Americans and the USA were at war.

7 Word focus *first*

a Look at the sentences. Is *first* a date (D) or a number (N)?

1 The first man in space was Yuri Gagarin.
2 Why was the first of May 1986 important?
3 The first American expedition to Everest was in 1963.

b Work in pairs. Ask and answer the questions.

1 Who was your first best friend?
2 When was your first day at school?
3 Where was your first job?
4 Who was your first boss?

Speaking

8 Look at these people. Are they from North America or South America?

George Washington   Tupac Amaru

Hillary Clinton   Pocahontas

Simón Bolívar   Robert E Lee

9 Now work in two pairs in a group of four. Talk about famous Americans.

Pair A: Turn to page 156.

Pair B: Turn to page 160.

THE FIRST AMERICANS

The Aztec Empire until about 1580

First Nations and Native Americans

The Maya

The Inca Empire until 1532

Geronimo: Apache hero
16 June 1829 – 17 February 1909

Today there are 23 countries in North, Central and South America. But five hundred years ago, a large area of South America – now Peru – was part of the Inca Empire. In Central America, the Maya people were important. And people in Mexico were part of the Aztec empire. In North America, there were different groups in different areas, for example the Apache, Navajo and Sioux. Today the name for these different groups is Native Americans (in the USA) or First Nations (in Canada). The leaders of these people are still famous today – the last Inca leader Tupac Amaru, the Aztec Moctezuma and the Apache war hero, Geronimo, for example.

The Apache people were from the south and west of North America. Geronimo was the grandson of an important Apache leader. He was born on 16 June 1829. When Geronimo was a young man, there was a war between Mexico and the USA, and the Native Americans. At that time, his family's land was part of Mexico. Now, it's part of the United States.

Geronimo was an Apache war hero. From 1886 until 1909 he was a prisoner of war in the United States. But he was also a famous celebrity. He was with President Theodore Roosevelt on 4 March 1905 – his first day as president.

celebrity (n) /sɪˈlebrɪti/ a person famous in their lifetime
land (n) /lænd/ area or nation
war (n) /wɔː/ conflict. For example: World War I 1914–1918.

10d I'm sorry

Vocabulary activities

1 Match the photos (a–f) with the words.

At nine o'clock yesterday I was … .
1 asleep   4 in traffic
2 at home   5 not well
3 busy   6 on the phone

2 Work in pairs. Ask and answer questions.

> *Were you at home at nine o'clock yesterday?*
>
> *Yes, I was.*
>
> *No, I wasn't.*

Real life apologising

3 🔊 **2.45** Listen to three conversations. Write the number of the conversation (1–3) next to the places.

a in a café   b in a classroom   c in an office

4 🔊 **2.45** Listen again. Complete the conversations with expressions for APOLOGISING.

1
T: Hello!
S: Hi, I'm sorry I'm late. [1] _____
T: That's OK. Take a seat.

2
R: Oh, hi Ravi.
C: Hi Clare.
R: Erm, the meeting was at 2.30. Where were you?
C: Oh, I'm sorry. [2] _____
R: [3] _____ It wasn't an important meeting.

3
A: Mmm, this coffee is good!
B: Yes, it is.
A: So, what about yesterday? We were at your house at ten o'clock. Where were you?
B: I'm very sorry. [4] _____ We were at my sister's house!
A: It's OK. [5] _____

> ▶ **APOLOGISING**
>
> | | |
> |---|---|
> | I'm (very) sorry. | We weren't at home. |
> | I'm sorry I'm late. | It's OK. |
> | The bus was late. | That's OK. |
> | I was (very) busy. | Don't worry. |

5 Pronunciation **sentence stress**

a 🔊 **2.46** Listen and repeat these sentences. Underline the word with the main stress.

1 I'm sorry I'm late.   3 I was very busy.
2 The bus was late.   4 We weren't at home.

b Work in pairs. Practise the conversations. Pay attention to sentence stress.

6 Work in pairs. Practise the conversations again. Use the vocabulary in Exercise 1.

> *Hello.*
>
> *Hi, I'm sorry I'm late. I was in traffic.*
>
> *That's OK.*

10e Childhood memories

Writing a blog

1 Work in pairs. Ask and answer the questions.

   1 Do you read blogs?
   2 What are the blogs about?
   3 Do you write a blog? What about?

2 Read Tyler's blog and answer the questions.

   1 When was he born?
   2 Where was he born?
   3 Where was his family's house?
   4 What was his favourite toy?
   5 Who were his friends?

3 What information does he give about these things?

   1 his parents and family
   2 his house
   3 his toys
   4 his friends

4 Writing skill *when*

a Complete these sentences from the blog.

   1 When I was a child, _____
   2 When I was ten, _____

b Find two more sentences with *when* in the blog.

c Rewrite these sentences as one sentence with *when*. Don't forget the comma.

   1 My parents were young. They weren't rich.
   2 My father was a student. He was poor.
   3 I was a child. I was happy.
   4 I was three years old. My sister was born.

5 Make notes about your childhood. Answer the questions in Exercise 2 for yourself. Make notes about the things in Exercise 3.

6 Use your notes and write two or three paragraphs about your childhood memories. Include a sentence with *When*.

7 Check your blog. Check the spelling, the punctuation and the verbs.

8 Work in pairs. Exchange blogs. Find one surprising thing in your partner's blog. Ask two questions about his or her childhood.

MY CHILDHOOD MEMORIES
Tyler Sanford

I was born on 4 July 1990 in Texas. My parents were teachers. When I was a child, my parents weren't rich. Our house was in a small town. It wasn't a big house. My family was small – me, my parents and my grandfather. My grandfather was old. He was kind and funny. But when he wasn't well, he wasn't happy.

I remember my favourite toy. It was a helicopter. It was a present from my grandfather. And I remember my first bicycle. It was red and it was fantastic. My friend Jack's bike was blue. When I was ten, my best friends were Jack and Nathan. They were in my class at school. We were bored at school. But when we were on holiday, it was great. We were typical boys!

10f The space race

The first American in space

Before you watch

1 Work in pairs. Look at the photo and the caption on page 126. Discuss these questions.

1 Who was the man in the photo?
2 What was the space race?
3 Why were the years 1957 and 1969 important?

2 💿 **2.47** Look at the word box. Listen and repeat the words.

3 Work in pairs. How many astronauts can you name? Where were they from?

While you watch

4 Watch the video without sound. How many times do you see these things?

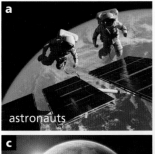
astronauts

a rocket launch

the Earth

the Moon

5 Watch the video. Check your answers from Exercise 1.

6 Work in pairs. Match the dates with the events.

Date	Event
1957	fire on Apollo 1
12 April 1961	men on the Moon
5 May 1961	Sputnik in space
20 February 1962	the first American in space
27 January 1967	the first person in space
20 July 1969	the first American to orbit the Earth

7 Watch the first part of the video again and check your answers from Exercise 6.

8 Work in pairs. Check your memory. Take turns to ask and answer these questions.

1 Who was president of the United States in 1961?
2 Who was Alan Shepard?
3 What was Sputnik?
4 What was the Mercury programme?
5 Who was John Glenn?
6 What was the Apollo programme?

9 Watch the video again and check your answers from Exercise 8.

10 Watch the second part of the video. Answer the questions.

1 What were Challenger and Columbia?
2 Which countries send astronauts to the International Space Station?

After you watch

11 Complete the sentences with *was, wasn't, were* or *weren't*.

1 President Kennedy's famous speech about space _____ in 1961.
2 The Soviet Union and the United States _____ in a space race.
3 Sputnik _____ part of the Soviet Union's space programme.
4 Alan Shepard, John Glenn and Gus Grissom _____ part of the Mercury programme.
5 On 27 January 1967, there _____ a fire on Apollo 1.
6 The first men on the Moon _____ Russian.

12 Work in groups. Write a list of five important events in the last ten years. Ask and answer the questions about the events.

- What was the date of the event?
- Where were you?
- Who were you with?

---

die (v) /daɪ/ Yuri Gagarin (1934–1968) He was born in 1934. He died in 1968.

a shuttle (n) /ˈʃʌtəl/

a fire (n) /ˈfaɪə/

the Soviet Union (n) /ðə ˈsəʊvɪət ˈjuːnjən/ the USSR

a goal (n) /gəʊl/ an aim

a speech (n) /spiːtʃ/ a person makes a speech when they speak at a public event

Mercury (n) /ˈmɜːkjʊri/ the first planet from the Sun

Sputnik (n) /ˈspʊtnɪk/ Soviet satellite

orbit (v) /ˈɔːbɪt/ to travel round the Earth in space

a success (n) /sək'ses/ a very good result of an activity

a programme (n) /ˈprəʊgræm/ work or tasks connected with one goal

a tragedy (n) /ˈtrædʒədi/ a terrible event

a satellite (n) /ˈsætəlaɪt/

Grammar

1 Complete the article about Bradley Wiggins with *was* or *wasn't*.

Bradley Wiggins: the first British winner of the *Tour de France*

Bradley Wiggins [1] _____ the first British winner of the *Tour de France*, but he [2] _____ born in Great Britain. He [3] _____ born in Belgium. Wiggins's mother [4] _____ English, but his father [5] _____ British – he [6] _____ Australian. Wiggins's father [7] _____ a professional cyclist. Wiggins's first medal [8] _____ at the Olympic Games in 2000 when he [9] _____ 20 years old. He [10] _____ third in the 2011 *Vuelta a España* and he [11] _____ the winner of the 2012 *Tour de France*.

2 Complete the sentences about the *Tour de France* with *was* or *were*.

1 The first race _____ in 1903.
2 The cyclists in 1903 _____ from France, Italy, Germany and Belgium.
3 The first winner five times in a row (1991–1995) _____ Miguel Indurain – a Spanish cyclist.
4 From 2006 to 2009 the winners _____ from Spain.
5 In 2011 the winner _____ Australian.
6 The British cyclist Chris Froome _____ second in the 2012 race.

3 Complete the questions about Bradley Wiggins with *was* or *were*.

1 Where _____ he born?
2 When _____ he born?
3 Where _____ his parents from?
4 What _____ his father's job?
5 How old _____ he in 2000?
6 Where _____ he in 2011?

4 Work in pairs. Ask and answer the questions in Exercise 3. Take turns.

I CAN	
talk about the past (*was/were*)	
say when people did things (time expressions)	

Vocabulary

5 Complete the sentences with ordinal numbers.

1 The _____ person in a race is the winner.
2 The person in _____ place gets a bronze medal.
3 May is the _____ month of the year.
4 August is the _____ month of the year.
5 October is the _____ month of the year.
6 The _____ of December is the last day of the year.

6 Complete the dates in the sentences with these words.

in   in   of   on   the

1 I was born on the third _____ June.
2 My sister was born _____ 1987.
3 My wife was born on _____ 27th of September.
4 My son was born _____ April.
5 My father was born _____ the 2nd of January, 1959.

7 Choose the correct option.

1 My first boss was very *nice / great*.
2 My sister is always *happy / fantastic*.
3 This TV presenter is very *great / interesting*.
4 Bradley Wiggins is a *famous / interesting* cyclist.
5 When I was a child, I wasn't *good / happy* at sports.
6 My maths teacher at school was nice and *fantastic / friendly*.

I CAN	
say dates	
describe people (adjectives)	
talk about activities	

Real life

8 Put the conversation in order.

a Don't worry. Are you OK now?
b Hello, Carolyn.   1
c Hi. Where were you this morning?
d Oh! I'm sorry. I wasn't well.
e The boss was here at nine o'clock.
f Why?
g Yes, thanks.

I CAN	
say where I was at different times	
make and accept apologies	

Speaking

9 Work in pairs. Choose two famous people. Prepare questions for an interview with these people.

10 Ask and answer your questions. Take turns.

Photo by Tim Laman

FEATURES

1 Work in pairs. Look at the photo. How many things can you name?

2 Work in pairs. Look at the captions (a–c). Which do you think is the correct caption for the photo? Why?

   a   An unusual campsite in the forests of Papua New Guinea.
   b   Police find a mystery object in a river in Papua New Guinea.
   c   A scientist discovers new plants in the forests of Papua New Guinea.

3 🔊 **2.48** Listen and check your ideas from Exercise 2.

4 🔊 **2.48** Listen again and complete the sentences.

   1   A large .... of these discoveries are in Indonesia.
   2   Scientists in Papua New Guinea usually find about two new plants or animals every ....
   3   Scientists sometimes arrive and leave by ....

5 Work in pairs. Can you name six animals and plants from your country?

11a The mystery of 'Ötzi' the Iceman

Reading

1 Read the article about an unusual discovery. Answer the questions.

1 Where were the tourists from?
2 Where were they in September 1991?
3 Where was the body?
4 What kind of investigation was it?

2 Read the article again. <u>Underline</u> the past forms (1–5) in the article. Then write the verbs next to the past forms.

1	was/were	*be*		be
2	went			find
3	found			go
4	took			have
5	had			take

Grammar **irregular past simple verbs**

3 Look at the grammar box. Then look at this sentence. Choose the correct option.

There is *only one / more than one* past simple form for each verb.

▶ IRREGULAR PAST SIMPLE VERBS
I/You He/She/It We/You/They   **went** for a walk.   **found** a body.
For further information and practice, see page 167.

4 Complete the sentences with these irregular past simple verbs.

found	had	took	went

1 The German tourists _____ to the police station.
2 The police _____ some arrows near the body.
3 The person _____ unusual shoes.
4 In 1998, scientists _____ the body to a museum of archaeology in Italy.

PART 1: THE DISCOVERY

The mystery of 'Ötzi' the Iceman

THE DISCOVERY In September 1991, two German tourists were on holiday in the Austrian Alps.

They went for a walk and they found a body in the ice. The body was very old – it wasn't the body of a mountaineer. The police took it to the University of Innsbruck in Austria.

This body was a mystery. Was it a man or a woman? Who was he or she? The person had an unusual knife and a bag with arrows. Where was he or she from? How old was the body? There were many questions. But this wasn't a police investigation. It was a scientific investigation.

Listening

5 🎧 2.49 Read these sentences. Then listen to part 2 of the Iceman's story: the investigation. <u>Underline</u> any information that is different.

1 The police started their investigation.
2 Scientists called the body 'Ötzi'.
3 He was about 65 years old.
4 He lived 10,000 years ago.
5 He died in winter.

6 🎧 2.49 Match the two parts of the sentences. Then listen again and check.

1 The scientists studied   from the north of Italy.
2 They finished   Ötzi.
3 Ötzi was   the body.
4 He walked   their report.
5 An arrow killed   to the mountains.

The Iceman at the South Tyrol Museum of Archaeology in Bolzano, Italy

The Iceman's knife

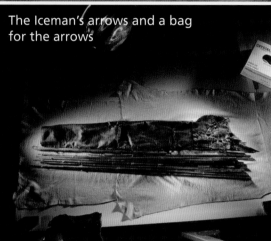

The Iceman's arrows and a bag for the arrows

Grammar regular past simple verbs

7 Look at the grammar box. What do we add to verbs to make the regular past simple form?

> **REGULAR PAST SIMPLE VERBS**

I/You	**studied** the body.
He/She/It	**called** him Ötzi.
We/You/They	**finished** their report.

For further information and practice, see page 167.

8 Pronunciation -ed verbs

🔊 **2.50** Listen and repeat the infinitive and past simple form of these verbs. Which verb has an extra syllable?

1	call	called	6	live	lived
2	die	died	7	start	started
3	discover	discovered	8	study	studied
4	finish	finished	9	walk	walked
5	kill	killed			

9 Write true sentences with this information.

Albert Einstein	died	from Germany.
Dian Fossey	had	gorillas in Africa.
John Lennon	lived	in 1980.
Marie Curie	studied	in North America.
Queen Victoria	was	nine children.
The Apache people	went	to university in Paris.

10 Complete the sentences. Use the past simple form of the verb.

1 My grandmother _____ (have) six children.
2 She _____ (die) in 1998.
3 My grandfather _____ (study) with Albert Einstein.
4 My cousin _____ (walk) across Australia in 2008.
5 My mother _____ (go) to university with JK Rowling.
6 I _____ (live) in Italy from 2009 to 2011.

Writing and speaking

11 Write sentences about you and your family with the verbs in Exercise 10. Write one false sentence.

My parents went to the South Pole in 2009.

12 Read your sentences to your partner. Can you discover the false sentence?

> My parents went to the South Pole in 2009.

> I think that's false!

TALK ABOUT ▶ YOUR FAMILY'S PAST ▶ WHAT DID YOU DO LAST YEAR? ▶ TELLING A STORY ▶ TALKING ABOUT THE PAST
WRITE ▶ AN EMAIL

131

11b Adventurers in action

Reading and listening

1 Read about Alastair Humphreys. Answer
the questions.

1 How old is he?
2 Where does he live?
3 What's his job?
4 How does he travel on his adventures?

2 Read the article on page 133. Circle three
regular past simple verbs. <u>Underline</u> the
past simple of these verbs.

| have | go | leave | see | meet | make |

3 🔊 **2.51** Listen to an interview with Jamie, a Twitter
follower of Alastair Humphreys. Put the sentences
in order.

a His friend made a video.
b He went swimming.
c They sent a video to Twitter.
d He watched a video.
e He drove to a lake.

4 🔊 **2.51** Can you remember? Why did Jamie go to the
lake? Listen again and check.

ADVENTURERS
IN ACTION!

5 Pronunciation *did you … ?*

🔊 **2.52** Listen and repeat these questions from the interview.

1 Did you watch Alastair's videos?
2 Did you like it?
3 Did you make a video too?

Grammar past simple negative and question forms

6 Look at the grammar box. Which auxiliary verb do we use to make questions and negatives in the past simple?

▶ **PAST SIMPLE NEGATIVE AND QUESTION FORMS**

I/You/He/She/It We/You/They	**didn't**	**leave** the UK.	
Did	I/you/he/she/it we/you/they	**walk?**	Yes, I/you/he/she/it/we/you/they **did**. No, I/you/he/she/it/we/you/they **didn't**.

For further information and practice, see page 168.

After ten years of international adventures, last year Alastair Humphreys stayed in the UK. He had a different kind of adventure: a 'local adventure'. He didn't go on a typical, dangerous trip. We asked him about his local adventure.

Tell us about your last adventure. Did you go to a dangerous place?

No, I didn't. I didn't leave the UK. I stayed in London. I went around London on the M25 motorway. But I didn't drive.

Did you walk?

Yes, I did. I left my house in London in January. It was cold and it was snowy. It wasn't easy. I saw new places. In fact, I saw some beautiful places. And I met interesting people. It was a local adventure.

And then what did you do?

I had one or two more local adventures and I made videos about them. People around the world watched the videos. But they didn't just watch them – they liked my ideas and they went on local adventures too.

ALASTAIR HUMPHREYS

DISCOVER YOUR LOCAL AREA
Age: 35
Home: London
Profession: British writer and adventurer

ADVENTURES:
2001–2005: cycling trip around the world
2008: *Marathon des Sables*
2009: across India on foot
2010: across Iceland

7 Look at the example. Then write questions about Alastair Humphreys.

Example:
cycle / around the world two years ago?

Did he cycle around the world two years ago?

1 run / a marathon in 2008?
2 walk across India / in 2009?
3 go to Iceland / last year?
4 swim / across the English Channel?
5 drive around the M25 / last year?
6 make videos / in 2006?

8 Work in pairs. Ask and answer the questions in Exercise 7.

Did he cycle around the world two years ago?

No, he didn't.

9 Write sentences about Alastair Humphreys with the information in Exercise 7.

He cycled around the world from 2001 to 2005.

Writing and speaking

10 Prepare a survey about last year. Write questions with these ideas.

• go on holiday
Did you go on holiday last year?
• stay in a hotel
• make a video
• leave your job
• drive to an interesting place
• meet an old friend
• send a message on Twitter
• swim in the sea

11 Work as a class. Find one name for each question.

Did you go on holiday last year?

Yes, I did. I went to Cairo.

12 Write sentences with the names.

José went to Cairo last year.

11c Discovering Madagascar

Reading

1 Look at the photos on page 135 and find:

> an animal   a plant   rocks

2 Work in pairs. Do you think these adjectives describe the things in the photos? Which things?

> beautiful   dangerous   fantastic
> interesting   unusual

3 Read the article on page 135. Answer the questions.

1 When did the writer go to Madagascar?
2 Who did he go with?
3 Why did they go to Madagascar?
4 What did they see there?

4 Read the last paragraph of the article again. Complete the sentences.

1 The writer fell on a _____ .
2 He cut his _____ .
3 He went to _____ .
4 A nurse cleaned his _____ .
5 She asked him a _____ .

5 Work in pairs. What did the nurse think about the trip? Do you agree with her?

Grammar past simple with question words

6 Look at the grammar box. Then look at the questions in Exercise 3. Which question words are in Exercise 3?

▶ PAST SIMPLE WITH QUESTION WORDS			
What			do?
Where			go?
When	did	I/you/he/she/it we/you/they	arrive?
Why			see?
Who			meet?
For further information and practice, see page 168.			

7 Look at the example. Then complete the questions with the correct *wh-* word.

Example:
When did he fall?

1 _____ did he cut?
2 _____ did he go?
3 _____ did he see there?
4 _____ did she say?

8 Work in pairs. Ask and answer the questions in Exercise 7.

9 **Word focus *with***

a Look at the pictures. Find and complete these two sentences from the article.

1 I was with a _____ .

2 We saw unusual white lemurs with _____ .

b Match the two parts of the sentences.

1 I booked my tickets with   a animals.
2 You can hitch-hike with   b a travel agent.
3 Vets work with   c my colleagues.
4 We saw a bird with   d Russian drivers.
5 I had lunch with   e unusual colours.

Speaking

10 Work in pairs. Can you remember the story of the writer's trip to Madagascar? Tell the story with these verbs. Take turns to say a sentence. You can use some verbs more than once.

> arrived   cleaned   cut   fell   saw   travelled
> walked   went

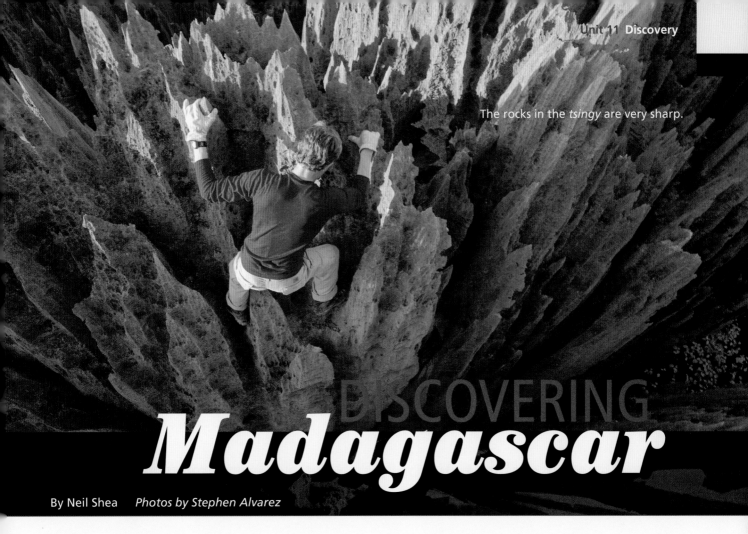

The rocks in the *tsingy* are very sharp.

DISCOVERING
Madagascar

By Neil Shea   *Photos by Stephen Alvarez*

I arrived in Madagascar in March, at the end of the rainy season. I was with a biologist and a photographer. We wanted to find some new species. We travelled to the park with our guide and after five days, we finally arrived there.

We walked through the *tsingy*. The rocks cut our clothes and our shoes too. It was very dangerous, but we saw hundreds of animals and plants. We saw beautiful birds and unusual white lemurs with red eyes. They didn't have any problems on the *tsingy* rocks!

Madagascar is a fantastic place. About 90 per cent of the animals and plants there live only in Madagascar. It's a very interesting place for scientists. There are some very unusual animals and plants in Madagascar's Tsingy de Bemaraha national park, but it's a dangerous place. The rocks – the 'tsingy' – in the park are very sharp. Neil Shea reports.

Then, one afternoon, I fell on a rock. I cut my leg. The cut was very deep. It took two days to reach the hospital. The nurse cleaned my leg. She looked at me. 'I have a question. Why did you go to the *tsingy*?' she asked. Then she said, 'It's very dangerous. I think you are a little crazy.' She didn't understand us. The *tsingy* is a natural paradise.

crazy (adj) /ˈkreɪzi/ not sensible

There are twenty-three types of this plant in the world. Eighteen of them are only in Madagascar.

This lemur lives only in Madagascar.

11d Did you have a good time?

Real life talking about the past

1 Work in pairs. Look at the photo. What can you see?

2 🎵 2.53 Listen to three conversations. Write the number of the conversation (1–3).

The people …
a had a meal.
b were in Sydney.
c didn't have a holiday.

3 🎵 2.53 Listen again and answer the questions for the conversations.

1 Did they stay at home?
2 Did they go swimming?
3 Did they pay for the meal?

> ▶ **TALKING ABOUT THE PAST**
>
> Did you have a good holiday last year?
> Did you have a good time in Sydney last week?
> Did you have a nice meal last night?
> Why not?
> There was a shark in the sea!
> We didn't go swimming.
> It was delicious.

4 Pronunciation *didn't*

a 🎵 2.54 Listen to three sentences from the conversations.

b 🎵 2.54 Listen and repeat the sentences.

5 Vocabulary time expressions

Look at these expressions. Which expressions did you hear in the conversations?

on Friday	last week	last year
last night	last weekend	yesterday

6 Work in pairs. Say one thing you did at each time in Exercise 5.

I had a nice meal on Friday.

7 Work in pairs. Look at page 174. Practise the conversations.

8 Work in pairs. First, choose an event for each time. Then take turns to ask and answer questions about the events. Say one thing you didn't do.

a day at the beach	last month
a holiday	last night
a meal	last week
a party	on Saturday
a trip	yesterday

Hi. Did you have a good day at the beach yesterday?

Yes, thanks, I did. But I didn't go in the water.

Why not?

It was very cold!

TALK ABOUT ▶ YOUR FAMILY'S PAST ▶ WHAT DID YOU DO LAST YEAR? ▶ TELLING A STORY ▶ **TALKING ABOUT THE PAST**
WRITE ▶ AN EMAIL

11e Thank you!

Writing an email

1 Work in pairs. Look at the photo. What's the situation?

2 Read the email to Lili. Choose the correct option (a–c).

a   Lili, Bibia and Mark went on holiday together.
b   Bibia and Mark visited Lili.
c   Lili visited Bibia and Mark.

> Dear Lili
>
> Thank you for a fantastic weekend! It was lovely to see you and we had a great time.
>
> On the way home we had a little adventure. (See attached photo!) … We got home late, but it was OK.
>
> Thanks again. Speak to you soon.
>
> Best wishes,
> Bibia and Mark

3 Read the parts of an email (a–c). Which part completes the email to Lili?

> **a** We missed the plane! So we found a hotel and stayed there for the night.
>
> **b** We got lost! We didn't have a map and so we went on the wrong road!
>
> **c** We had a problem with the car! We called my dad. After an hour, he arrived and helped us.

4 Writing skill expressions in emails

a Look at the expressions. Which expressions do we use to start (S) an email? Which expressions do we use to end (E) an email? Write S or E next to the expressions.

> All the best,
> Best wishes,
> Dear
> Hi
> Love,
> Regards,

b Complete this email from Toni to Celia with expressions from Exercise 4a.

> 1 _____
>
> Thanks for your help yesterday. I found my car keys when I got home!
>
> See you soon.
>
> 2 _____

5 Work in pairs. Your partner is your friend. How did you help your friend? Each person choose one of these situations. Tell your partner.

- You helped your friend when he/she lost his/her phone.
- You helped your friend when he/she didn't have any money.
- You sent your friend some photos.
- Your friend had a meal at your house.

6 Write a 'thank you' email to your friend for his/her help in the situation in Exercise 5.

7 Check your email. Check the past simple verbs.

8 Exchange emails with your friend. Ask a follow-up question about your friend's email.

An unusual plant in the Madagascan forest

Before you watch

1 Work in pairs. Answer the questions.

1 What perfumes do you know or like?
2 Do you use perfume?
3 Where do perfumes come from?

2 💿 **2.55** Look at the word box. Listen and repeat the words.

3 Work in pairs. Are these sentences about Madagascar true (T) or false (F)? What do you think?

1 Madagascar is an island.
2 There are some unusual plants in the forests.
3 It's an interesting place for scientists.
4 It's easy to travel into the forests by car.

While you watch

4 Watch the video without sound. Tick (✓) the things you see.

a forest	a laboratory
scientists	a shop
flowers	some fruit
a river	some animals
a balloon	the sea

5 Read two summaries of the video. Then watch the video with sound. Choose the correct summary (a or b).

a Some scientists discovered a new flower.
They made a new perfume.
They sold the perfume in Madagascar.

b Some scientists went to Madagascar.
They looked for plants and flowers.
One of the scientists found two new plants.

6 Read the sentences. Then watch the video again. Are the sentences true (T) or false (F)?

1 Roman Kaiser and Willi Grab are from Switzerland.
2 They make perfumes.
3 Their laboratory is in Madagascar.
4 They found plants with black fruit.
5 Willi Grab didn't like the taste of the fruit.

7 Work in pairs. Which option or options (a–c) are true?

1 Why did the scientists go to Madagascar?
  a because there are a lot of interesting plants
  b because they go there every year
  c because they wanted to find new plants

2 What did the scientists see in Madagascar?
  a some interesting animals
  b some beautiful flowers
  c some unusual fruit

After you watch

8 Match the two parts of the sentences.

1 The scientists went to Madagascar
2 They travelled into
3 Then they flew in
4 They looked for
5 They cut the fruits and
6 They studied the new scents
7 Last year, this scientist found two

a a balloon.
b in the laboratory.
c interesting flowers and fruits.
d the forest by boat.
e they tasted them.
f last year.
g new plants.

9 Work in pairs. Read the sentences in Exercise 8.

Student A: Read the first part of the first sentence.

Student B: Read the second part of the first sentence.

Take turns.

10 Work in pairs.

Student A: You are a scientist. You went to Madagascar.

Student B: You are a journalist.

Ask and answer questions with *when, where, what, who* and *why* about the trip to Madagascar.

Take turns.

acidic (adj) /əˈsɪdɪk/ Lemons taste acidic.	**man-made** (adj) /ˌmænˈmeɪd/ the opposite of natural, made by people
a balloon (n) /bəˈluːn/	**a perfume** (n) /ˈpɜːfjuːm/ For example: Chanel No. 5, CK One.
a chemist (n) /ˈkemɪst/ a type of scientist	**a scent** (n) /sent/ a natural perfume – some flowers have nice scents
close (adj) /kləʊs/ similar	**stephanotis** (n) /ˌstefəˈnəʊtɪs/ a type of flower
earthy (adj) /ˈɜːθi/ similar to soil or earth	**taste** (v) /teɪst/ to try or eat a small part of some food
a flower (n) /ˈflaʊə/	**watery** (adj) /ˈwɔːtəri/ with a lot of water
juicy (adj) /ˈdʒuːsi/ with a lot of juice – mangoes are juicy	

Grammar

1 Complete the blog with the past simple forms of the verbs.

Field notes

A blog by National Geographic *expeditions*

Last month, I was with a group of people on a boat. We ¹_____ (be) in Alaska. Justin Hofman, a scuba diver, ²_____ (be) in the water. He ³_____ (have) a camera. He ⁴_____ (take) pictures under the sea. He ⁵_____ (send) video pictures to us on the boat. It was very exciting! We ⁶_____ (see) beautiful animals and plants. There was an audio connection too – Justin ⁷_____ (talk) about the animals and plants and we ⁸_____ (ask) him questions. It was a great experience.

Posted by Carly

2 Read the blog again. Are the sentences true (T) or false (F)? Change the verb to the negative form to make the false sentences true.

1 Carly went to Canada.
2 She was on a bus.
3 She had a camera.
4 Justin Hofman took photos.
5 Carly saw interesting things.
6 She answered questions about animals.

3 Read Carly's answers. Write the questions.

1 No, I didn't go into the water.
2 Yes, I had a great time.
3 No, I didn't take any photos.
4 I went with my friends.

4 Work in pairs. You were on the boat in the photo. Ask and answer questions with these words.

1 Where / go?   4 Who / talk to?
2 When / arrive?   5 Why / go?
3 What / see?

I CAN	
talk about the past (irregular and regular past simple verbs)	
ask and answer questions about the past (question words)	

Vocabulary

5 Read about David's day. Complete the sentences with eight of these verbs.

cleaned	cut	drove	fell	finished	found
made	met	paid	sent	swam	took

Yesterday

1 I _____ breakfast.
2 I _____ my room.
3 I _____ twenty euros in my room.
4 I _____ a text message.
5 I _____ to a café.
6 I _____ my friend Alex.
7 He _____ a photo of us.
8 I _____ for lunch.

6 Write true sentences for you with six of the verbs from Exercise 5 and time expressions.

Last night / weekend / week / month / year
On Monday / Tuesday, etc.

7 Work in pairs. Read your sentences. Did you do the same things?

I CAN	
talk about people's lives	
say when people did things	

Real life

8 Read the conversation between two colleagues. Choose the best option.

A: Did you have *a good day at the beach / a nice meal / a good holiday* last night?
B: No, I didn't.
A: Oh? Why not?
B: The food was delicious, but my friend *missed the plane / saw a shark in the sea / cut her hand with her knife*!
A: Oh no!

I CAN	
talk about the past	
give reasons for events in the past	

Speaking

9 Work in pairs. Practise the conversation in Exercise 8 with the other two options.

Unit 12 The weekend

A group of women in Chengdu, China
Photo by Cary Wolinsky

FEATURES

1 Work in pairs. Look at the photo of women on their day off work. What days do you work or study?

2 🎵 2.56 Work in pairs. Look at the photo again and discuss the questions. Then listen and check your ideas.

1 What day of the week do you think is the women's day off?
2 What do you think they usually do on their day off?
3 What days do you think are the weekend in China?

3 🎵 2.56 Listen again. Write the weekend days for these countries. What about your country?

Oman: _____ , _____
Egypt: _____ , _____

4 Work in pairs. What do you do at the weekend? Do you stay at home, do you go out or do you work?

I work on Saturday and on Sunday I stay at home.

12a At home

Vocabulary **rooms in a house**

1 Look at the things (1–5) there are in different rooms. Write the rooms next to the things.

> bathroom   bedroom   dining room   ~~kitchen~~
> living room

1   a fridge, an oven — *kitchen*
2   a chair, a table — ....
3   an armchair, a sofa — ....
4   a bed, a wardrobe — ....
5   a bath, a shower, a toilet — ....

2 🎵 **2.57** Listen and check your answers from Exercise 1.

3 🎵 **2.58** Listen and repeat the words for the rooms.

4 Work in pairs. Tell your partner one thing about each room in your home.

> *We don't have a dining room. We eat in the kitchen.*

> *My kitchen is very small.*

HOME LIFE
PHOTO PROJECT

We asked our readers to take photos of the important things in their homes.
This week, we show Ayu Malik's photos. It's Saturday morning in her home in Sumatra, Indonesia.

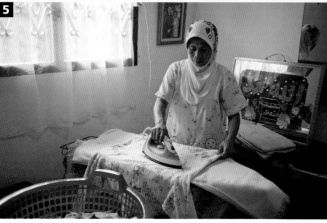

Listening

5 Look at the photos (1–6) of a family at home in Indonesia. Which rooms are the people in?

6 🔊 **2.59** Match the sentences with the photos. Then listen and check.

  a They're drinking coffee.
  b He's playing a computer game with his son.
  c He's bathing his daughter.
  d They're washing their motorbikes.
  e She's making lunch.
  f She's ironing.

7 🔊 **2.59** Listen again and say who the people are. Write next to the sentences in Exercise 6.

  Example:
  a They're drinking coffee.
  Ayu's father and his friend

Grammar **present continuous**

8 Look at the grammar box. Then look at the sentences in Exercise 6. Which auxiliary verb do we use to make the present continuous?

▶ PRESENT CONTINUOUS AFFIRMATIVE and NEGATIVE		
I	am (not)	**sitting** on the floor. **making** lunch. **ironing**.
You/We/They	are (not)	
He/She/It	is (not)	
For further information and practice, see page 168.		

9 Complete the sentences about the photos on page 142.

  Example:
  1 ___*Ayu's mother*___ is cooking.
  2 _____ are smiling.
  3 _____ are sitting on mats.
  4 _____ is lying on the sofa.
  5 _____ is standing near a window.
  6 _____ is wearing an orange T-shirt.

10 Look at the photos again and write true sentences. Use the negative form when necessary.

  Example:
  1 Ayu's mother /eat
     Ayu's mother isn't eating.
  2 Amir / play with his daughter
  3 Ayu's father and his friend / read a book
  4 Amir's brother / watch TV
  5 Ayu's sister / do homework
  6 Ayu's brother and his friend / wash their cars

11 Look at these questions from the conversation with Ayu Malik. Which photos are the questions about?

  a What's she making?
  b Are they sitting outside or inside?
  c What are they doing?
  d Are they reading?

12 Work in pairs. Ask and answer the questions in Exercise 11.

▶ PRESENT CONTINUOUS QUESTIONS and SHORT ANSWERS			
(What)	Am	I	**reading**? **doing**?
	Are	you/we/you/they	
	Is	he/she/it	
Yes, **I am**. No, **I'm not**. Yes, **she/he/it is**. No, **she/he/it isn't**. Yes, **you/we/you/they are**. No, **you/we/you/they aren't**.			
For further information and practice, see page 168.			

13 Look at the photo of Ayu's family in the living room. Write questions. Then ask and answer the questions with your partner.

  Example:
  children / watch TV?
  Are the children watching TV?

  1 boy / lie on the sofa?   3 women / wear scarves?
  2 man / sit on a chair?   4 girls/ sit on the floor?

Speaking

14 Work in groups. Show some photos on your mobile phone to the group. Take turns to ask and answer questions.

> *Who's that?*

> *That's my cousin and her husband.*

> *What are they doing?*

> *They're singing.*

12b Next weekend

Vocabulary **weekend activities**

1 Look at the photo. Where are the people? What are they doing?

2 Read the *At the weekend* questionnaire. Are the activities at home (H) or out of the home (O)?

3 Work in pairs. Do the questionnaire. Is your weekend similar or different from your partner's?

> *I never get up late at the weekend.*

> *I sometimes get up late.*

At the weekend

How often do you do these weekend activities? Always? Sometimes? Never?

	me	my partner
get up late		
go out for a meal		
go for a walk		
go shopping		
go to a concert		
go to the cinema		
go to a museum		
have a party		
meet friends		
play football		
read the newspaper		
visit family		

A busy shopping centre on a typical Saturday

Listening

4 🎵 **2.60** Look at the information about three events. Then listen to a conversation between two friends. Tick (✓) the events they talk about.

5 🎵 **2.60** Listen again. Answer the questions.

1 When is Lauren going shopping?
2 Why is she going shopping?
3 Who is giving a talk at the Natural Science Museum?
4 What is Alex doing on Sunday?

6 Pronunciation *going* and *doing*

a 🎵 **2.61** Listen to five sentences from the conversation. Notice the /w/ sound in *going* and *doing*.

b 🎵 **2.61** Listen and repeat the sentences.

Grammar **present continuous with future time expressions**

7 Look at the sentences from the conversation in Exercise 4 in the grammar box. Are the speakers talking about now or a time in the future?

> ▶ **PRESENT CONTINUOUS WITH TIME EXPRESSIONS**
>
> What are you doing **this weekend**?
> Sports Gear is having a sale **tomorrow**.
> She's giving a talk about her trip **on Sunday evening**.
>
> For further information and practice, see page 168.

8 🎵 **2.62** Look at the information for the City Hall in Exercise 4. Write the conversation between Alex and Oscar. Then listen and check.

A: What / you / do / this weekend?
O: *I'm not sure.*   My sister / come / tomorrow.
A: she / stay the weekend?
O: *Yes, she is.*   We / go / to a party on Saturday.
A: *Does she like music?*   The West Country Folk Band / play at the City Hall on Sunday.
O: *OK. Great!*

Speaking

9 Make a diary for next weekend. Write activities for these times.

Saturday

MORNING	
AFTERNOON	
EVENING	

Sunday

MORNING	
AFTERNOON	
EVENING	

10 Work in pairs. Ask and answer questions about next weekend. Are you doing the same things?

> *What are you doing on Saturday morning?*

> *I'm going shopping with my sister. What about you?*

12c A different kind of weekend

Reading

1 Look at the photos on page 147. Answer the questions.

1 What do you think the people are doing?
2 Where do you think they are?
3 Do you think there is anything unusual about them?

2 Read the article and check your ideas from Exercise 1.

3 Read the article again. Are the sentences true (T) or false (F)?

1 Joel Connor works for free at the weekend.
2 He's a builder.
3 He's building a house for his family.
4 He works with his friends.
5 He's coming to Greensburg next weekend.

4 Look at the photos on page 147. Complete the sentences.

1 Joel is moving a large ....
2 .... are working on the roof.
3 Jill Eller is standing near ....
4 Jill's holding a part of ....

5 Match a verb in A with words in B. Check your answers in the article.

A	B
build	people
help	a house
know	a project
start	people
work	in an office

Grammar **tense review**

6 Look at these three sentences from the article. Underline the verbs. Then write past (P), present (PR) or future (F) next to the sentences.

1 Joel Connor works in an office in Kansas.
2 The community started a project.
3 Jill is standing near her new house.
4 Next weekend, Joel is moving to a different project.

7 Add these expressions to the sentences.

> In this photo
> From Monday to Friday
> Last year

1 ...., Joel Connor works in an office in Kansas.
2 ...., the community started a project.
3 ...., Jill is standing near her new house.

8 Word focus *do*

a Match the questions (1–5) with the answers (a–e).

1 What do you do?
2 What are you doing?
3 What do you usually do at the weekend?
4 What did you do at the weekend?
5 What are you doing at the weekend?

a I'm going to a concert with a friend.
b I'm a builder.
c I visited my cousin in London.
d I'm making lunch.
e I meet my friends.

b The verb *do* is a main verb and an auxiliary verb. Look at the questions. Underline the main verbs and circle the auxiliary verbs.

c Work in pairs. Ask and answer the questions in Exercise 8a.

> *What do you do?*
>
> *I'm a ...*

Speaking

9 Work in groups. Plan a special weekend for a person you all know. Then tell the class.

> *Next weekend is our special weekend for Tracey. On Saturday morning, we're all going shopping. Then Tracey is having a beauty makeover.*

A different kind of weekend

Joel Connor works in an office in Kansas. His job is a typical nine-to-five, Monday-to-Friday job. So at the weekend, he does something different. He does voluntary work. He helps different organisations and people for free. Every weekend, there's a new project. This weekend, Joel is helping to build a house. You can see him in the photo. He's moving a large blue panel. It's part of a wall. Joel isn't a professional builder, but that's the interesting thing about this project. The other people are 'weekend builders' too.

These 'weekend builders' are from the small town of Greensburg in Kansas. A year ago, a tornado hit their town. After the tornado, the community started a project to build new homes. The project is for 30 new homes. They have help from a building company and a group of volunteers.

Joel says, 'I heard about the tornado and the new project. I knew some people in Greensburg. I wanted to help.' Joel's friends are here this weekend too. They're on the roof. They're working with Jill and Scott Eller. Jill and Scott are building their 'dream house'. Jill (right) is standing near her new house. She's holding a part of the new wall. They're making the house 'tornado-resistant' – that's why it has an unusual shape.

The Ellers' house is almost ready, so next weekend, Joel is moving to a different project. Why does he do voluntary work? 'I have time, I can help people, I make friends and it's fun! So why not?' he says.

dream house /n/ /ˈdriːm haʊs/
  a house you'd like a lot
tornado /n/ /tɔːˈneɪdəʊ/ a very windy
  storm
tornado-resistant /n/ /tɔːˈneɪdəʊ-
  rɪˈzɪstənt/ a tornado can't hurt this

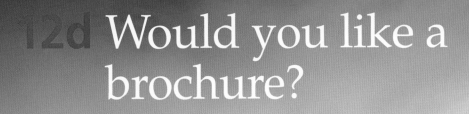

12d Would you like a brochure?

Vocabulary **weekend trips**

1 Complete the sentences. There is one extra word.

| brochure | court | exhibition | museum | return ticket |

1 You look at pictures in an _____ .
2 You play tennis on a _____ .
3 You read a _____ .
4 You buy a _____ to go to a place and come back.

Real life **buying tickets**

2 🔊 **2.63** Listen to three conversations (a–c). Match the number of tickets with the place and the price.

Number of tickets	Place	Price
a four	a castle	6 pounds
b three	a museum	10 pounds
c two	a tennis court	21 pounds

3 🔊 **2.63** Listen again. Are the sentences true (T) or false (F)?

a 1 There are four children.
    2 They take a brochure in French.

b 3 They buy single tickets.
    4 They are going to the castle and gardens.

c 5 People are playing on all the tennis courts.
    6 They buy a ticket for two hours.

4 Pronunciation *would you ... ?*

a 🔊 **2.64** Look at the expressions for BUYING TICKETS. Listen and repeat the questions.

b Work in pairs. Ask and answer questions with *Would you like ... ?*

a single ticket
to play football
a drink
to go to the museum

> ▶ **BUYING TICKETS**
>
> Four tickets for the museum, please.
> Three return tickets to Lindisfarne, please.
> Would you like a brochure for the *Home Life* exhibition?
> Would you like it in English?
> Would you like to buy the tickets now?

5 Work in pairs. Look at the audioscript on page 174. Practise the conversations.

6 Work in pairs. Buy and sell tickets.

Student A: Turn to page 156.

Student B: Turn to page 160.

TALK ABOUT ▶ YOUR PHOTOS ▶ NEXT WEEKEND ▶ A SPECIAL WEEKEND ▶ **BUYING TICKETS** WRITE ▶ AN INVITATION

12e Join us for lunch

Writing an invitation

1 Read the invitation. Answer the questions.

1 Why are Estefania and Tim celebrating?
2 How are they celebrating?
3 When is it?
4 Where is it?
5 What do you think *RSVP* means?

2 Read the replies to the invitation. How many people are coming to the party?

1
> Estefania, thank you for the invitation to lunch. My sister is arriving from Canada on 4 April, so I can't come! Briony

2
Today at 18:51 PM   Pete:
> Hi Tim. Thanks for the invitation. I'm coming!

3
> Hi Estefania. We'd like to come to lunch, but Bill is swimming in his club competition. Can we come late? Is that OK?
> Ronnie and Steve

4
> Dear Estefania and Tim
>
> Thank you very much for your invitation. We had a great time when we saw you last year. We are travelling to London on 4 April, so we can't make it this time. Sorry!
>
> Dani and Eve

5
> Hi Stef and Tim
> Thank you for the invitation. I'd like to come. Why don't I bring a cake? See you on 4 April!
> Gabi

ESTEFANIA AND TIM ARE MOVING HOUSE!

PLEASE JOIN US FOR LUNCH

ON SUNDAY 4 APRIL AT 2 P.M.

OUR NEW ADDRESS IS 3 FORD STREET
                    BAMBRIDGE

RSVP STEF@ROUNDHOUSE.NET

---

3 Writing skill **spelling: verb endings**

a Read the invitation and the replies again. Write the forms of the verbs.

1 move ....
2 arrive ....
3 come ....
4 swim ....
5 travel ....

b How does the spelling of these verbs change in the present continuous?

c Complete the table. Make sure you spell the verbs correctly.

	Present continuous	Present simple (*he/she/it*)	Past simple
do	*doing*	*does*	*did*
drive			
fly			
lie			
make			
see			
sit			
smile			
study			

4 Write an invitation to an event (a party, a picnic, a trip) to celebrate the end of the course.

5 Check your invitation. Check the spelling.

6 Exchange invitations with somone in your class. Read your classmate's invitation. Can you go to this event? Write a reply. If you can't go, give a reason. Give the reply to your classmate.

12f Saturday morning in São Tomé

This fisherman doesn't work on Saturdays.

Before you watch

1 Work in pairs. Ask and answer these questions.

1 Can you play a musical instrument?
2 Can you paint or draw?
3 Do you go fishing?
4 Can you swim?

2 🔘 **2.65** Look at the word box. Listen and repeat the words.

3 Work in pairs. Look at these people. What do they do at the weekend? Make true sentences about the people.

People	Activities
Children Farmers Fishermen Musicians Shop assistants	do homework. give concerts. go to school. go to the market. meet friends. play music. play with friends. rest. sing songs.

4 Work in pairs. Look at the people in Exercise 3 again. What do these people do at the weekend in your country?

5 São Tomé is the captial of São Tomé and Principe. How many islands are there in the country?

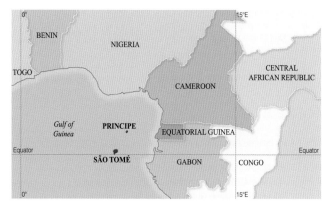

While you watch

6 These things are in the video. Watch the video again and put the pictures in order.

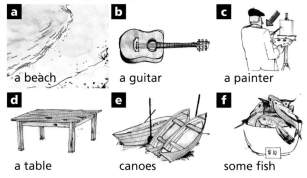

a a beach   b a guitar   c a painter
d a table   e canoes   f some fish

7 Watch the video again and write down one thing about each person.

1 Oswaldo Santos
2 Guillerme Carvalho
3 Nezo

8 Work in pairs. Compare your answers from Exercise 7.

9 Watch the video again and answer the questions.

1 Who is playing in the water?
2 Who is resting in a boat?
3 Who is buying fish?
4 Who is playing the guitar?
5 Who is singing?
6 Who is painting?

10 Work in pairs. Ask and answer the questions in Exercise 9. Do you agree?

After you watch

11 Complete the text with these words.

art	colours	concert	guitar	life	music
musician	painters	people	song		

Oswaldo is a ¹ _____ . He's in a group called *Grupo Tempo*. He plays the ² _____ , he sings and he writes ³ _____ .

Oswaldo, Guillerme and Nezo are playing a new ⁴ _____ . They're giving a ⁵ _____ next week.

Guillerme and Nezo are ⁶ _____ too. They paint things from local life – the ⁷ _____ , the ⁸ _____ and the animals. Their music and ⁹ _____ is about ¹⁰ _____ in São Tomé.

12 Make notes about musicians or artists you like.

13 Work in pairs. Tell your partner about the person or people in Exercise 12.

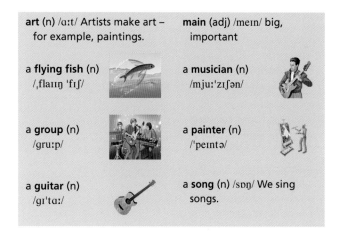

art (n) /ɑːt/ Artists make art – for example, paintings.

main (adj) /meɪn/ big, important

a flying fish (n) /ˌflaɪɪŋ ˈfɪʃ/

a musician (n) /mjuːˈzɪʃən/

a group (n) /gruːp/

a painter (n) /ˈpeɪntə/

a guitar (n) /gɪˈtɑː/

a song (n) /sɒŋ/ We sing songs.

UNIT 12 REVIEW

Grammar

1 Look at the photo of people at a bus stop in Santiago, Chile. Match these words (1–5) with the people (a–e). Then write sentences with the present continuous.

1 make / a phone call
2 wear / a brown jacket
3 hold / some books
4 talk / to her friend
5 walk / to the bus stop

2 Complete the paragraph about the photo with the correct form of the present continuous.

It's Friday evening in Santiago. These people
¹ _____ (stand) at a bus stop. There's a
bus at the bus stop. The bus doors ² _____
(open), but the people ³ _____ (not get) on
it. They ⁴ _____ (wait) for different buses.
Some of the people ⁵ _____ (go) home. They
⁶ _____ (think) about the weekend. Some
⁷ _____ (not go) home – they ⁸ _____
(take) the bus to work.

3 Put the words in a telephone conversation in order.

A: *Oh hello.* you / what / doing /are / ?
B: office / I / leaving / the / am / .
A: *Really?* late / is / it / .
B: *I know.* this / working / we / late / are / week / .
A: *OK.* to / coming / you / tomorrow / the beach / are / ?
B: *I don't know.* are / going / time / you / what / ?
A: leaving / at /are /eleven o'clock / we / .
B: friend / is / coming / your / ?
A: *Yes, he is.*
B: *OK. Great.*

Vocabulary

4 Work in pairs. Where do people do these things? Ask and answer questions about rooms with these words.

1 make meals?   4 watch TV?
2 sleep?   5 eat?
3 have a shower?   6 read?

5 Match a verb from A with words from B.

A	B
get up	to the cinema
go	to a concert
go	family
go	football
go	friends
have	late
meet	the newspaper
play	a party
read	shopping
visit	for a walk

6 Work in pairs. Tell your partner about the things you usually do at the weekend. Do you do similar things?

Real life

7 Match the requests (1–4) with the responses (a–d).

1 A return ticket to Oxford.
2 Three tickets for the concert, please.
3 Two tickets for Cinema One, please.
4 Two tickets for the castle, please.

a Two adults? That's fifteen pounds please.
b Here you are. Would you like an audio commentary?
c Are you coming back today?
d Would you like to sit upstairs or downstairs?

Speaking

8 Work in pairs. Tell your partner about your plans. What are doing next weekend/week/month?

UNIT 1a, Exercise 16, page 11

Student A

1 Listen to your partner. Write the jobs.

a ....   c ....

b ....   d ....

2 Spell these jobs to your partner.

e   driver   f   artist

g   photographer   h   writer

UNIT 2b, Exercise 13, page 25

Student A

1 Look at the photo. You are on holiday in Oman. Look at the sentences (1–4) and choose an option. Then have a telephone conversation with your friend (Student B) about your holiday.

1   You're *OK / happy*.
2   It's *hot / cold*.
3   The beach is *nice / beautiful*.
4   Your hotel is *nice / OK*.

2 Your friend (Student B) is on holiday. Prepare questions with these words. Then have a telephone conversation with Student B.

1   where?   4   city / beautiful?
2   OK?   5   hotel / nice?
3   cold?

UNIT 3b, Exercise 10, page 37

Student A

1 Look at the information about photo A. Answer your partner's questions about this photo.

Ivan
Miroslava
in Russia
Miroslava's sister
Ivan's 23 and Miroslava's 21

2 Look at photo B. Ask your partner about this photo. Ask questions with *who, where, what* and *how old*.

UNIT 4b, Exercise 10, page 49

Student A

1 Look at the information about photo A. Answer your partner's questions about this tower.

2 Look at photo B. Ask your partner about this tower. Ask the questions on page 49.

- The Space Needle tower
- It's in Seattle in the United States.
- It's open every day of the year.
- It's a symbol of Seattle. It's in Hollywood films, for example, *Sleepless in Seattle*.

Unit 5c, Exercise 8, page 62

Student A

1 Tell your partner about this microwave oven. Use *can* and *has*.

shopping_online.com

EasyCook Microwave

Product features:
cook and heat food ✓
3 power options ✓
make cakes ✗
digital clock ✓
buy online ✓

2 Listen to your partner. Make notes (1–5) about this microwave oven.

ProfessionalChef Microwave

1 ....
2 ....
3 ....
4 ....
5 ....

3 Look at the two microwave ovens. Do you think they are cheap or expensive?

Unit 6c, Exercise 10, page 74

Student A

1 Look at the photos and the information about sports events 1 and 3. Ask your partner five questions about events 2 and 4. Complete the information. You get 5 points if you identify the event after one question, 4 points if you ask two questions, etc.

		1 Wimbledon	**2**	**3** the Dakar Rally	**4**
1	**Where?**	London		South America	
2	**When?**	June and July		January	
3	**What kind of event?**	a competition		a race	
4	**Prize?**	money		–	
5	**Sport?**	tennis		motor sport	

2 Look at the information about Wimbledon and the Dakar Rally. Answer your partner's questions.

Unit 8c, Exercise 9, page 98

Student A

Write the questions (1–3). Note your answers to the questions.

Then ask your partner the questions. Note your partner's answers. Then check the results on page 157.

Quiz

Are you a 'morning person' or an 'evening person'?

1: you / wake up before your alarm clock?

  a yes   **b** no   **c** sometimes

2: you / always have breakfast?

  a yes   **b** no   **c** it depends

3: It's midnight. Where / you?

  a in bed   **b** at my computer   **c** it depends

UNIT 9b, Exercise 12, page 109

Student A

1 Look at this room. Answer Student B's questions.

2 Look at these two rooms. Student B has one of these rooms. Ask questions to identify the room. Use *Is there a ... ?* and *Are there any ... ?*

UNIT 10c, Exercise 9, page 122

Pair A

1 Listen to Pair B. Who are the people?

2 Look at the notes. Tell Pair B about these two people. Don't say the names.

Date of birth	1595
Place of birth	Virginia, North America
Biographical information	a prisoner of the English married to an English farmer, John Rolfe
Name	Pocahontas

Date of birth	19 January 1807
Place of birth	Virginia, North America
Biographical information	leader, the Confederate army of Virginia, American Civil War also was in war between Mexico and the USA
Name	Robert E Lee

UNIT 12d, Exercise 6, page 148

Student A

1 You work in the ticket office at the City Museum. Look at this information and listen to Student B. Answer his/her questions.

Great Explorers Exhibition

Tickets: adults £2.50; children £1.50

Brochures: £2.00

Audio information: English, French, German, Spanish

2 You are a group of two adults and four children. You are going to Bambridge Castle. Ask Student B questions to find out the time of the last bus and ticket prices.

Buses to Bambridge Castle
Every hour 9.15 – _____
Tickets: single £ _____ ; return £ _____
Return ticket + entry to castle £ _____

UNIT 1a, Exercise 16, page 11

Student B

1 Spell these jobs to your partner.

a filmmaker   b engineer

c doctor   d teacher

2 Listen to your partner. Write the jobs.

e ....
f ....
g ....
h ....

UNIT 2b, Exercise 13, page 25

Student B

1 Your friend (Student A) is on holiday. Prepare questions with these words. Then have a telephone conversation with Student A.

1 where?   4 beach / beautiful?
2 OK?   5 hotel / nice?
3 cold?

2 Look at the photo. You are on holiday in New York. Look at the sentences (1–4) and choose an option. Then have a telephone conversation with your friend (Student A) about your holiday.

1 You're *OK / happy*.
2 It's *hot / cold*.
3 The city is *nice / beautiful*.
4 Your hotel is *nice / OK*.

UNIT 3b, Exercise 10, page 37

Student B

1 Look at photo A. Ask your partner about this photo. Ask questions with *who, where, what* and *how old*.

2 Look at the information about photo B. Answer your partner's questions about this photo.

John
Anna
in Alaska, USA
the wedding official
John's 28 and Anna's 27

Unit 8c, Exercise 9, page 98

Are you a 'morning person' or an 'evening person'?

Results

Mostly 'a': You are a morning person. Evening activities are difficult for you. Good jobs for you are jobs in offices and in business.

Mostly 'b': You are an evening person. Morning activities are difficult for you. Good jobs for you are jobs in hospitals, the arts and the media.

Mostly 'c': You are not a morning person or an evening person. This group of people is the majority.

UNIT 4b, Exercise 10, page 49

Student B

1 Look at photo A. Ask your partner about this tower. Ask the questions on page 49.

2 Look at the information about photo B. Answer your partner's questions about this tower.

- The Minaret of the Samarra Mosque
- It's in Samarra in Iraq.
- It's not open to tourists at the moment.
- The spiral shape is famous. Samarra is a UNESCO World Heritage Site.

Unit 5c, Exercise 8, page 62

Student B

1 Listen to your partner. Make notes (1–5) about this microwave oven.

EasyCook Microwave

1 ....
2 ....
3 ....
4 ....
5 ....

2 Tell your partner about this microwave oven. Use *can* and *has*.

shopping_online.com

ProfessionalChef Microwave

Product features:
memory (100 options) ✓
10 power options ✓
cook and heat food ✓
make cakes ✓
buy online ✓

3 Look at the two microwave ovens. Do you think they are cheap or expensive?

Unit 6c, Exercise 10, page 74

Student B

1 Look at the information about the New York Marathon and the Masters. Answer your partner's questions.

	1	2 the New York Marathon	3	4 the Masters
1 Where?		New York		Georgia, USA
2 When?		November		April
3 What kind of event?		a race		a competition
4 Prize?		money		money, a green jacket
5 Sport?		running		golf

2 Look at the photos and the information about sports events 2 and 4. Ask your partner five questions about events 1 and 3. Complete the information. You get 5 points if you identify the event after one question, 4 points if you ask two questions, etc.

Unit 8c, Exercise 9, page 98

Student B

Write the questions (4–6). Note your answers to the questions.

Then ask your partner the questions. Note your partner's answers. Then check the results on page 157.

Are you a 'morning person' or an 'evening person'?

 4: What time / you / get up at the weekend?

a early   **b** late   **c** the same time as usual

5: What / the main meal of the day for you?

a lunch   **b** dinner   **c** it depends

6: you / fall asleep in front of the TV in the evening?

a yes   **b** no   **c** sometimes

UNIT 9b, Exercise 12, page 109

Student B

1 Look at these two rooms. Student A has one of these rooms. Ask questions to identify the room. Use *Is there a ... ?* and *Are there any ... ?*

2 Look at this room. Answer Student A's questions.

UNIT 10c, Exercise 9, page 122

Pair B

1 Look at the notes. Tell Pair A about these two people. Don't say the names.

Date of birth	24 July 1783
Place of birth	Caracas, South America
Biographical information	married to a Spanish woman: Maria Teresa
	leader of four countries: Colombia, Venezuela, Ecuador, and Bolivia
	first president of Venezuela
Name	Simón Bolívar

Date of birth	22 February 1732
Place of birth	Virginia, North America
Biographical information	leader, the American army, War of Independence
	first president, USA
Name	George Washington

2 Listen to Pair A. Who are the people?

UNIT 12d, Exercise 6, page 148

Student B

1 You are a group of two adults and three children. You are English and one of the children is German. Visit the Great Explorers Exhibition at the City Museum. Ask Student A questions to find out ticket and brochure prices and about audio information.

> *Great Explorers Exhibition*
> *Tickets: adults £_____ ; children £_____*
> *Brochures: £_____*
> *Audio information: English, _____,*
> *_____ , Spanish*

2 You work in the ticket office at the bus company. Look at this information and listen to Student A.

Buses to Bambridge Castle

Every hour 9.15 – 18.15

Tickets: single £4.25; return £7.00

Return ticket + entry to castle £8.50

UNIT 1

a/an (articles)

a + single noun with consonants: *b, c, d, f,* etc.
a d<u>r</u>iver, **a** f<u>i</u>lmmaker
an + single noun with vowels: *a, e, i, o, u*
an <u>a</u>rtist, **an** <u>e</u>ngineer

Practice

1 Complete the sentences with *a* or *an*.

1 I'm _____ scientist.
2 I'm _____ writer.
3 I'm _____ explorer.
4 I'm _____ artist.
5 I'm _____ photographer.
6 I'm _____ student.

I + am, you + are

I	am ('m)	John.
You	are ('re)	a student.

Practice

2 Complete the sentences with *I'm* or *You're*.

1 ALEX: _____ Alex.
   MIREYA: Hi, Alex.
2 ROBERT: _____ Mattias Klum.
   MATTIAS: Yes.
3 CAROLYN: Hi!
   ALEX: _____ Carolyn.
4 MIREYA: Hello.
   ROBERT: Hi! _____ Robert Ballard.
5 MATTIAS: Hello! _____ Mattias.
   CAROLYN: Hi, Mattias.
6 ALEX: I'm a photographer.
   ROBERT: _____ Alex Treadway.

he/she/it + is

He	is ('s)	French.
She	is ('s)	from Japan.
It	is ('s)	in Italy.

Practice

3 Write sentences with *He's*, *She's* and *It's*.

1 Dechen / from Ladakh
2 Manu / Nepalese
3 Dechen / Indian
4 Jagat / in Nepal
5 Manu / from Jagat
6 Ladakh / in India

I + am, you + are, he/she/it + is (be)

I	am ('m)	John.
You	are ('re)	a student.
He	is ('s)	French.
She	is ('s)	from Japan.
It	is ('s)	in Italy.

Practice

4 Complete the sentences with *am, are* and *is*.

1 Hi! I _____ Elena.
2 Paul _____ an engineer.
3 He _____ from Hong Kong.
4 It _____ in China.
5 You _____ English.
6 I _____ Mexican.

my, your

I'm Jared. **My** name's Jared.
You're Maria. **Your** name's Maria.

Practice

5 Complete the sentences with *my* and *your*.

1 _____ name's Ludmilla. I'm from Russia.
2 Hello! You're my teacher. _____ name's Mr Jones. I'm Tomas.
3 Hello! _____ name's Paolo.
4 Hi. I'm Juan. What's _____ name?
5 '_____ mobile number is 695 836 736.'
   'Thanks.'
6 'John, what's _____ home number?'
   'It's 0352 497 268.'

UNIT 2

we/they + are

We	are ('re)	in Canada.
They	are ('re)	from Brazil.
		Italian.

Practice

1 Complete the sentences.

1 This is Jack. This is Bill. _____ are Canadian.
2 France and Spain _____ in Europe.
3 Bruno and Paola are from Italy. _____ Italian.
4 I'm with my teacher. _____ 're in a classroom.
5 I'm from Japan. My friend is from Japan. _____ Japanese.
6 Jane and Barry are Australian. _____ 're from Australia.

be

I	am ('m)	
You	are ('re)	
He		
She	is ('s)	in Canada.
It		from Brazil.
We		Italian.
You	are ('re)	
They		

Practice

2 Choose the correct option.

1 My name is Carlos and I *am / is / are* a student.
2 Toshiba *am / is / are* Japanese.
3 You *am / is / are* a student.
4 My teacher *am / is / are* from London.
5 I'm with my friend. We *am / is / are* in China.
6 Germany and France *am / is / are* in Europe.

be negative forms

I	am not ('m not)	
You	are not (aren't)	a teacher.
He		from Europe.
She	is not (isn't)	in China.
It		
We		from Europe.
You	are not (aren't)	in China.
They		

Practice

3 Rewrite the sentences with the verb in the negative form.

1 Jack's a student.
2 We are Spanish.
3 Bolivia is in Europe.
4 I'm happy.
5 Susana and Gina are from Peru.
6 You're a writer.

be questions and short answers

		Yes, I **am**.
Are you		No, I'm **not**.
	in a hotel?	Yes, she/he/it **is**.
Is she/he/it	nice?	No, she/he/it **isn't**.
	from Peru?	Yes, we/you/they **are**.
Are we/you/they		No, we/you/they **aren't**.

Practice

4 Write questions with the correct form of *be*. Then write two answers for each question with *yes* and *no*.

1 Simona / from Bolivia?
2 John / a teacher?
3 you / on holiday?
4 your hotel / nice?
5 Paris / beautiful?
6 Susana and Gina / in Paris?

plural nouns

Add -*s*.
a friend → friends

Change -*y* to -*ies*.
a city → cities

Add -*es* to nouns that end in -*s*, -*ch* and -*ss*.
a bus → buses

Practice

5 Write the plural of these nouns.

1	a lake	5	a beach	9	a student
2	a country	6	a photo	10	a holiday
3	a car	7	a mountain	11	an island
4	an airport	8	a tent	12	a phone

UNIT 3

possessive 's

Alexandra is Philippe's daughter.
Simone and Jacques are Alexandra's grandparents.

Note: The possessive *'s* is not a contraction of *is*.
Who's Fabien? = Who is Fabien?
He's my brother. = He is my brother.
He's Jean-Michel's son. = He is Jean-Michel's son.

Practice

1 Look at the family tree. Write sentences.

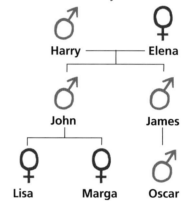

1 James / Oscar / father
2 John and James / Elena / sons
3 Lisa and Marga / Harry / granddaughters
4 Lisa / Marga / sister
5 Elena / Oscar / grandmother
6 James / John / brother

his, her, our, their

	my	
	your	
	his	
This is		friend.
	her	
	our	
	their	

Practice

2 Choose the correct option.

1 This is a photo of my brother at *her / his* wedding.
2 My wife is Russian. *Her / My* name is Olga.
3 We are happy. It's *his / our* daughter's wedding.
4 Hi, Zara. Is it *her / your* birthday today?
5 My parents are on holiday. It's *his / their* wedding anniversary.
6 Her name is Anna. What's *her / your* husband's name?

irregular plural nouns

a child → children
a man → men
a woman → women
a person → people

Remember: Add -s or -es and change -y to -ies to make regular plural nouns.

Practice

3 Complete the singular and plural nouns.

1 How old are the wom_____ in the photo?
2 Who are the pe_____ at the wedding?
3 This chil_____ is three years old.
4 Who is the pe_____ in this photo?
5 James and Eliza are my chil_____ .
6 Our teacher is a m_____ .

UNIT 4

prepositions of place

next to   in   near   opposite

*The museum is **next to** the market.*
*The market is **in** London Street.*
*The cinema is **near** the bank.*
*The café is **opposite** the bus station.*

Practice

1 Look at the picture. Complete the sentences.

1 The bank is _____ the hotel.
2 The bank is _____ the Tourist Information Centre.
3 Two people are _____ the park.
4 The car park is _____ the hotel.
5 The Science Museum is _____ the car park.
6 Three people are _____ the cinema.

this, that

This book is in French.

That's Big Ben!

Use *this* for things near to you. Use *that* for things not near to you.

Practice

2 Look at the picture in Exercise 1. Read the words of the people in the park (1–3) and of the people in the street (4–6). Choose the correct option.

1 'This / That park is nice.'
2 'This / That is my bank.'
3 'Is this / that your book?'
4 'This / That is a beautiful street.'
5 'Look. Is this / that café open?'
6 'Is this / that your car in the car park?'

question words

What's that?   **Why's** Big Ben famous?
Where's the bank?   **Who's** this?
When's the park open?   **How old** is he?

Practice

3 Match the questions (1–6) with the answers (a–f).

1 Where's Luton airport?
2 What's your address?
3 How old is your brother?
4 Who's that in the park?
5 When are banks open in your country?
6 Why's the tower famous?

a From Monday to Friday.
b It's very old.
c It's near London.
d 36, Oxford Street.
e My sister and her children.
f He's 27.

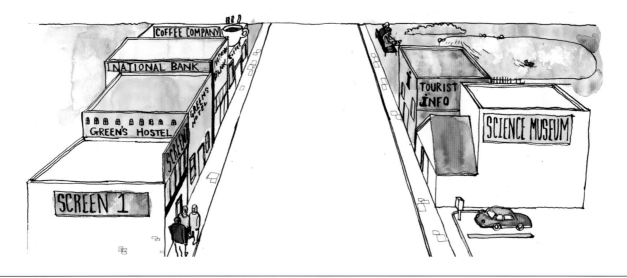

UNIT 5

can/can't

Affirmative		Negative	
I/You He/She/It We/You/They	**can** cook.	I/You He/She/It We/You/They	**can't** cook.

can't = cannot

Practice

1 Choose the correct option.

1 Babies *can / can't* run.
2 Children *can / can't* see.
3 Babies *can / can't* move.
4 Cars *can / can't* fly.
5 Children *can / can't* run.
6 Animals *can / can't* speak.

can questions and short answers

Questions			Short answers		
Can	I/you he/she/it we/you/they	cook?	Yes, No,	I/you he/she/it we/you/they	**can.** **can't.**

Practice

2 Write questions and answers.

1 he / sing ✓
2 you / drive a car ✓
3 they / play table tennis ✗
4 she / cook ✗
5 we / speak English ✓
6 it / swim ✗

have/has

I/You We/You/They	**have**	a mobile phone.
He/She/It	**has**	batteries.

Practice

3 Complete the sentences with *have* and *has*.

1 I _____ two cameras.
2 My laptop _____ a webcam.
3 My friends _____ three children – they're all boys.
4 We _____ a French car.
5 My city _____ three parks.
6 My sister _____ a great job – she's a computer engineer.

adjective + noun

My **headphones** are **new**.
I have **new headphones**.
Note: Adjectives have only one form: *I have ~~news~~ headphones*.
The word order is adjective + noun, NOT noun + adjective: *I have ~~headphones new~~*.

Practice

4 Put the words in order to make sentences.

1 is / camera / this / Japanese / a
2 fantastic / phone / my / a / memory / has
3 MP3 player / you / great / a / have
4 city / Paris / beautiful / a / is
5 red / a / my / has / sister / car
6 is / Jack's / man / an / grandfather / old

very, really

	This camera is It's	expensive. great/fantastic.	
	This camera is It's	**really** **very** **really** ~~very~~	expensive. great/fantastic.

5 Rewrite the sentences with *very* or *really* where possible.

1 This laptop is light. (really)
2 Their house is big. (very)
3 My friend's new phone is fantastic. (really)
4 This is a good oven. (very)
5 That microwave is great. (very)
6 We have an old car. (really)

UNIT 6

like

Affirmative
I/You/We/You/They **like** fruit.

Negative
I/You/We/You/They **don't like** vegetables.
(don't = do not)

Practice

1 Write sentences with the correct form of *like*.

1 I / basketball ☹
2 we / rugby ☺
3 they / tennis ☺
4 you / tea ☹
5 I / coffee ☺
6 they / cake ☹

like questions and short answers

Questions				Short answers
Do	I you we you they	**like**	pizza?	Yes, I/you/we/you/they **do.** No, I/you/we/you/they **don't.**

Note:
'Do you like pizza?' 'Yes, I do.' NOT *'Yes, I ~~like~~.'*

Practice

2 Write questions with the words. Then write answers to the questions.

1 cheese / they ✓
2 fruit / you ✗
3 meat / you ✓
4 fish / they ✓
5 rice / they ✗
6 eggs / you ✗

he/she + like

Affirmative		Negative	
He	likes books.	He	doesn't like music.
She		She	
		(doesn't = does not)	

Questions			Short answers
Does	he	like fish?	Yes, he/she **does**.
	she		No, he/she **doesn't**.

Practice

3 Four of these sentences have a missing word: *does* or *doesn't*. Rewrite the sentences with the missing word.

1 Zeb likes Arizona.
2 Joanna like action films.
3 your teacher like music?
4 Ryan like swimming.
5 Elise like sports?
6 Krishnan likes coffee.

object pronouns

Diana likes	me.
	you.
	him.
	her.
	it.
	us.
	you.
	them.

Practice

4 Look at the underlined nouns. Complete the sentences with an object pronoun.

1 I like birds, but my friend doesn't like
   ....
2 We can't see you. Can you see .... ?
3 She's a popular writer, but I don't like
   ....
4 Do you like pop music? Yes, I love ....
5 Matt Damon is fantastic in the *Bourne* films. I love ....
6 I have a cat. It loves ....

UNIT 7

present simple I/you/we/you/they

Affirmative			Negative		
I			I		
You			You		
We	speak	Sami.	We	don't speak	Sami.
You			You		
They			They		
			(don't = do not)		

Practice

1 Rewrite the sentences in the form given in brackets.

1 I live near a beach. (negative)
2 You don't have a car. (affirmative)
3 My friends speak English. (negative)
4 I don't understand Japanese. (affirmative)
5 We study in the holidays. (negative)
6 They live in a tent. (negative)

present simple questions I/you/we/you/they

Questions				Short answers
Do	I			Yes, I/you/we/you/they **do**.
	you	live	in Sweden?	
	we			No, I/you/we/you/they **don't**.
	you			
	they			

Practice

2 Write questions with the words. Then write answers to the questions.

1 in Egypt (you / live) ✓
2 to college (they / go) ✗
3 Spanish (I / study) ✓
4 English (your friends / learn) ✓
5 friends in this class (we / have) ✓
6 at this school (you / teach) ✗

present simple with question words

What			do?
Where			
Who	do	I/you/we/you/they	go?
Why			meet?
When			

Practice

3 Read the questions and answers. Complete the questions with a question word.

1 '.......................... do you do?'
   'I work in a school.'
2 '.......................... do you have your holidays?'
   'In summer.'
3 '.......................... do you do in the summer holidays?'
   'I play golf.'
4 '.......................... do you play golf with?'
   'I play golf with my brothers.'
5 '.......................... do your brothers live?'
   'They live near me.'
6 '.......................... do you play golf?'
   'I like it.'

UNIT 8

present simple *he/she/it*

Affirmative		Negative	
He/She	**gets up** at 7:30	He/She	**doesn't work.**
		(doesn't = does not)	

Add -*s*.
get up → *gets up*

Add -*es* to verbs that end in -*ch* and -*sh*.
teach → *teaches, finish* → *finishes*

The verbs *go, do* and *have* are irregular.
go → *goes, do* → *does, have* → *has*

Practice

1 Write the correct form of the verb in brackets.

1 Kristen _____ (get up) at seven o'clock.
2 She _____ (not / go) to work in the day.
3 She _____ (work) in the evening.
4 She _____ (not / work) in a school.
5 She _____ (teach) adults at a college.
6 She _____ (start) work at 5.30 and she _____ (finish) at ten o'clock.

prepositions of time

at + time	**at** 6.30
on + day	**on** Tuesday/Tuesdays
in + part of day, month, season	**in** the morning, **in** July, **in** summer

Note: *at night*

Practice

2 Complete the text with the correct preposition.

Alain works in the city. He gets home ¹ _____ seven o'clock ² _____ the evening. He has dinner ³ _____ 8.30 and ⁴ _____ winter he watches TV. He goes out for dinner ⁵ _____ Fridays. He can go to bed late because he doesn't work ⁶ _____ Saturdays.

frequency adverbs

100%
I **always** have breakfast.
We **usually** get up early.
My friend **often** works late.
I **sometimes** travel in my job.
My friend **never** writes emails.
0%

Note: The word order is adverb + verb, except with *be*: *I am never late*, NOT *I ~~never am~~ late*.

Practice

3 Put the words in order to make sentences.

1 in the morning / coffee / have / usually / I
2 travels / colleague / my / in her job / often
3 homework / never / our / gives / teacher / us
4 always / I / at night / read
5 studies / my / at home / friend / sometimes
6 my brother / late / always / works

present simple questions *he/she*

Questions			Short answers
Does	he she	teach?	Yes, he/she **does.** No, he/she **doesn't.**
Questions with question words			
What does he/she **do?**			
Where does he/she **go** in summer?			

Practice

4 Read the sentence. Then write a question with the words in brackets.

1 Carl doesn't have breakfast at 7.30. (8.30 ?)
2 Anna doesn't finish work at 6.30. (what time ?)
3 Julia doesn't go to bed late. (early ?)
4 Michael doesn't work in an office. (where ?)
5 My brother doesn't read novels. (what ?)
6 My sister doesn't like tea. (coffee ?)

How … ?

How does he take photos?
How many people do you work with?
How often does your friend telephone you?
How old is that tiger?
How much is this book?

Practice

5 Read the sentence. Then write a question with the words in brackets and an expression with *How* … .

1 I have 200 friends on Facebook. (you ?)
2 I'm 23. (you ?)
3 This camera is $99. (that camera ?)
4 I phone my sister every day. (your sister ?)
5 I take videos with my phone. (you ?)
6 I make coffee with milk. (you ?)

UNIT 9

there is/are

Singular	Plural
There's a book in my bag. (There is)	**There are** some books in my bag.

Practice

1 What's in my suitcase? Write sentences.

1 a map ✓
2 clothes ✓
3 books ✓
4 a camera ✓
5 keys ✓
6 a pair of sandals ✓

there is/are negative and question forms

Negative singular	Negative plural
There isn't a bus. (There is not)	**There aren't** any hotels. (There are not)
Questions and short answers singular	**Questions and short answers plural**
Is there a sofa? Yes, **there is.** No, **there isn't.**	**Are there** any trains today? Yes, **there are.** No, **there aren't.**

Practice

2 What's in my suitcase? Write questions. Then write answers to the questions.

1 a hat ✗   4 a phone ✓
2 a passport ✓   5 pairs of shoes ✓
3 pens ✗   6 tickets ✗

imperative forms

Book the hotel online.
Don't travel by bus.
(don't = do not)

Practice

3 Read the instructions from a travel guide for some tourists. Choose the best option.

1 *Don't forget / Forget* your passports.
2 *Don't arrive / Arrive* at the airport on time.
3 *Don't give / Give* me your mobile numbers, please.
4 *Don't be / Be* late.
5 *Don't wait / Wait* a moment, please.
6 *Don't switch off / Switch off* your phone on the plane.

UNIT 10

was/were

Affirmative
I/He/She/It **was** Russian.
You/We/You/They **were** Russian.

Practice

1 Complete the paragraph with *was* or *were*.

Sally Ride [1] _____ the first American woman in space. She [2] _____ born in 1951. Her parents [3] _____ from California. Her first space flight [4] _____ in 1983. She [5] _____ the writer of five books for children. They [6] _____ about space and science.

was/were negative and question forms

Negative
I/He/She/It **wasn't** famous.
You/We/They **weren't** famous.
(wasn't = was not, weren't = were not)

Questions		Short answers
Was	I he she it	happy at school?	Yes, I/he/she/it **was**. No, I/he/she/it **wasn't**.
Were	you we you they		Yes, you/we/you/they **were**. No, you/we/you/they **weren't**.

Practice

2 Complete the sentences with *was, wasn't, were* and *weren't*.

1 '_____ Neil Armstrong the first man in space?'
    'No, he _____ .'
2 My parents are from Hong Kong. They _____ born in Europe.
3 My mother is a doctor. She _____ the first woman in her family with a university degree.
4 '_____ you born in 1986?'
    'Yes, I _____ .'
5 '_____ the first televisions in colour?'
    'No, they _____ .'
6 I _____ very good at music at school and I can't play a musical instrument.

UNIT 11

irregular past simple verbs

Affirmative	
I/You/He/She/It/We/You/They	**went** to the Alps. **had** a good holiday.

do → did, find → found, go → went, have → had,
leave → left, make → made, see → saw, take → took

Practice

1 Complete the sentences with the past simple form of the verb.

1 We _____ (take) a lot of photos on our holiday.
2 The tourists _____ (go) for a walk.
3 I _____ (have) lunch at home yesterday.
4 We _____ (see) a great film last week.
5 I _____ (make) dinner last night.
6 My father _____ (leave) school when he was fourteen.

regular past simple verbs

Affirmative
I/You/He/She/It/We/You/They **walked** in the mountains.

Add *-ed* or *-d*.
start → started, live → lived

Change *-y* to *-ied*.
study → studied

Practice

2 Complete the sentences with the past simple form of the verb.

Last weekend we [1] _____ (go) for a walk in the mountains. We [2] _____ (start) early in the morning. We [3] _____ (walk) for two hours. Then we [4] _____ (have) a snack. We [5] _____ (find) a bag on the walk. We [6] _____ (finish) our walk and we [7] _____ (take) the bag to the police station. The police [8] _____ (discover) a lot of money in the bag.

past simple negative and question forms

Negative
I/You/He/She/It/We/You/They **didn't go** on holiday last year.

Questions
Did I/you/he/she/it/we/you/they **drive**?

Short answers
Yes, I/you/he/she/it/we/you/they **did**.
No, I/you/he/she/it/we/you/they **didn't**.
(didn't = did not)

Note: In the negative and in question forms, we use the past simple of *do* (*did*) + verb (*go, drive*, etc.), NOT
They didn't ~~went~~ on holiday last year.
Did they ~~went~~ on holiday last year?

Practice

3 Complete the interview with an explorer.

Q: ¹ _____ (you / travel) a lot last year?
A: Yes, I ² _____ . I went to 17 countries.
Q: Wow! ³ _____ (you / go) to South America?
A: Yes, we did. We walked and we cycled across Ecuador, Peru and Chile. We ⁴ _____ (use) public transport.
Q: ⁵ _____ (you / write) a blog about your trip?
A: No, I ⁶ _____ , but I made some videos for a new website.

past simple with question words

Questions with question words			
What			see?
Who			
Where	did	I/you/he/she/it/we/you/they	
When			go?
Why			

Practice

4 Write questions for these answers. Use a question word and the correct form of the <u>underlined</u> verb.

1 We <u>met</u> lots of interesting people.
2 They <u>went</u> to Cancun in Mexico.
3 She <u>saw</u> some beautiful buildings.
4 We <u>arrived</u> at the hotel at night.
5 I <u>went</u> there because I like the food.
6 They <u>stayed</u> in a youth hostel.

UNIT 12

present continuous

Affirmative / Negative		
I	am / 'm not	cooking.
He/She/It	is / isn't	eating.
We/You/They	are / aren't	reading.

We use the present continuous for activities in progress at the time of speaking.

Practice

1 Write sentences about an English class with the correct form of the verb in brackets.

1 The teacher _____ (talk).
2 Olga and Ludmilla _____ (not write).
3 I _____ (listen).
4 Juan and Paolo _____ (read).
5 Tomas _____ (not watch) a video.
6 Ana _____ (not look) out of the window.

Questions			Short answers		
Am	I			I	am.
			Yes,	he/she/it	is.
				we/you/they	are.
Is	he/she/it	cooking?			
				I	'm not.
Are	we/you/they		No,	he/she/it	isn't.
				we/you/they	aren't.

Practice

2 Write questions with these words. Use the information in Exercise 1 to answer the questions.

1 Ana / look out of the window
2 Tomas / watch a video
3 I / listen
4 Olga and Ludmilla / write
5 the teacher / talk
6 Juan and Paolo / read

present continuous with future time expressions

	tomorrow.
I'm meeting my friends	on Saturday (morning).
	this/next weekend.
	on 8 June.

We use the present continuous + future time expressions for future plans.

Practice

3 Read each sentence. Does it refer to now (N) or the future (F)?

1 I'm playing tennis on Sunday.
2 We aren't watching this TV show.
3 My friends are coming this weekend.
4 Is your family having a party tonight?
5 What are you doing in June?
6 My sister is staying with us.

Unit 1

🔊 1.1
Hi! I'm Mike.

🔊 1.2
M: Hi. I'm Mattias. I'm a filmmaker.
C: Hi. I'm Carolyn. I'm a writer.
R: Hello. I'm Robert. I'm an explorer.
M: Hi. I'm Mireya. I'm a scientist.
A: Hello. I'm Alex. I'm a photographer.

🔊 1.4
1 I'm a photographer.
2 I'm a doctor.
3 I'm a teacher.
4 I'm an artist.
5 I'm an engineer.
6 I'm a driver.

🔊 1.5
A: Hello.
C: Hi.
A: I'm Alex Treadway.
C: Oh, you're a photographer!
A: Yes.

🔊 1.6
Y: Hi.
M: Hello. I'm Mattias Klum.
Y: Oh, you're a filmmaker!
M: Yes, for *National Geographic*.

🔊 1.8
1 P: I'm Paola.
   Q: Can you spell that?
   P: Yes. P–A–O–L–A.
2 B: I'm Bryan.
   Q: Can you spell that?
   B: Yes. B–R–Y–A–N.
3 S: I'm Sean.
   Q: Can you spell that?
   S: Yes. S–E–A–N.
4 A: I'm Ana.
   Q: Can you spell that?
   A: Yes. A–N–A.

🔊 1.9
Manu is from Nepal. He's Nepalese.
Dechen is from India. She's Indian.

🔊 1.10
Brazil	Brazilian
Canada	Canadian
China	Chinese
Egypt	Egyptian
France	French
Germany	German
Great Britain	British
Italy	Italian
Japan	Japanese
Mexico	Mexican
Oman	Omani
Spain	Spanish
the United States	American

🔊 1.12
1 Toshiba is Japanese.
2 Curry is from India.
3 Judo is Japanese.
4 Flamenco is from Spain.

🔊 1.13
1 Africa   5 North America
2 Asia   6 South America
3 Australia
4 Europe

🔊 1.15
one   four   five   eight   nine

🔊 1.16
Jamaica   Brazil
France   Great Britain
the Dominican Republic

🔊 1.17
A: What's your phone number?
B: My mobile number is 619 408 713.
A: 6–1–9 4–0–8 7–1–3. OK! And what's your work number?
B: It's 01661 467928.
A: 0–1–6–6–1 …
B: … 4–6–7–9–2–8.
A: Great. Thanks.

🔊 1.18
Hi.   Goodnight.
Hello.   Goodbye.
Good morning.   Bye.
Good afternoon.
Good evening.

🔊 1.19
R: Good morning. What's your name, please?
L: Hi. My name's Schultz.
R: Can you spell that?
L: Yes. S–C–H–U–L–T–Z: Schultz.
R: What's your first name?
L: Liam: L–I–A–M.
R: Thank you. What's your job?
L: I'm a photographer. I'm from *Today* magazine.
R: OK. Sign here, please.
L: OK. Thanks. Bye.
R: Goodbye.

🔊 1.21
Y: Hi, Katya. How are you?
K: Fine, thanks. And you?
Y: I'm OK. This is Silvia. She's from Madrid.
K: Nice to meet you, Silvia.
S: Nice to meet you too.

Unit 2

🔊 1.23
This is in Fiji. It's an island. It's morning.

🔊 1.25
1 This is Jane. This is Paul. They're Australian.
2 I'm Meera. This is Suri. We're from India.
3 In this photo I'm with my friend, Jack. We're in Egypt.
4 Laura is with Brad, Andy and Jessica. They're on holiday.
5 Jeanne and Claude are from France. They're French.
6 I'm happy. My friend is happy. We're happy!

🔊 1.26
We're in Egypt.   They're on holiday.
We're from India.   They're Australian.
We're happy.   They're French.

🔊 1.27
1 We aren't in Tunisia.
2 It isn't a beach.
3 Brad isn't on the camel trek.
4 I'm not in this photo.

🔊 1.29
zero   thirty   sixty   ninety
ten   forty   seventy one hundred
twenty   fifty   eighty

🔊 1.30
a It's twelve degrees in London today.
b Phew! It's hot! It's thirty-five degrees today.
c It isn't hot. It's eighteen degrees.
d It's twenty-seven degrees here.
e Wow! It's thirty-six degrees in Sydney today.
f Brrr. It's cold. It's thirteen degrees here.

🔊 1.31
G: Hi! Where are you now? Are you in France?
L: Yes, I am. I'm in the Alps. It's beautiful!
G: Are you OK?
L: No, I'm not. It's two degrees!
G: Wow! Is it cold in your hotel?
L: No, it isn't. The hotel is nice.
G: It's thirty-six degrees in Sydney today.
L: Oh! That's hot!
G: Are Kara and Ona in France?
L: No, they aren't. They're on a beach in Morocco!

🔊 1.32
1 Q: Are you OK?
   A: Yes, I am.
2 Q: Is Kara in France?
   A: No, she isn't.
3 Q: Are you and Paul in Sydney?
   A: Yes, we are.
4 Q: Is Greg in London?
   A: No, he isn't.
5 Q: Are Kara and Ona in Morocco?
   A: Yes, they are.
6 Q: Is your hotel nice?
   A: Yes, it is.

🔊 1.33
1 red   5 black   9 white
2 blue   6 orange   10 grey
3 yellow   7 brown
4 green   8 pink

🔊 1.34
1 In Cuba, cars are old.
2 In London, buses are red.
3 In Hawaii, beaches are black.
4 In Iceland, the lakes are hot.
5 Lake Geneva is in two countries – Switzerland and France.
6 The Blue Mountains are in Australia.
7 Hong Kong, Shanghai and Beijing are cities in China.
8 John Lennon, Charles de Gaulle and John F Kennedy are airports.

🔊 1.37
1 My car registration number is PT61 APR.
2 My email address is jamesp@national.org.
3 My address is 3 Park Street, Gateshead.
4 My postcode is NE2 4AG.

🔊 1.38
A: Good evening.
S: Good evening. My name's Sato. This is my ID.
A: Thank you. Where are you from, Mr Sato?
S: I'm from Tokyo.
A: Ah! Is this your address?
S: Yes, it is.

A: What's the postcode?
S: It's 170–3293.
A: OK. Are you on holiday here?
S: No, I'm not. I'm on business.
A: What's your telephone number in the UK?
S: It's 0795 157 963.
A: Thanks. Is this your email address?
S: Yes, it is: e p sato at hotmail dot com.
A: OK. Sign here, please. Here are your keys.
S: Thanks. What's the car registration number?
A: It's with your keys – BD61 ATR.
S: Thanks.

Unit 3

1.41
Danvir and Mohan are brothers. Ravi and Danvir are father and son. Ravi and Mohan are father and son.

1.42
brother   son   father   parents
sister   daughter   mother

1.43
Alexandra Cousteau is part of a famous family. She's Jacques Cousteau's granddaughter. Jean-Michel Cousteau is Jacques Cousteau's son. He's a filmmaker. Jean-Michel's children are Fabien and Celine. Fabien's a marine explorer. Celine's an explorer. Jean-Michel's brother Philippe is dead. Philippe's children are Alexandra and Philippe Jr. Alexandra's an environmentalist. Her brother is an environmentalist too. And Alexandra's grandmother Simone was the first woman scuba diver.

1.44
1 Altan is Batu's mother.
2 Altan is Odval's daughter.
3 Kushi is Altan's granddaughter.
4 Odval is Batu's grandmother.

1.45
E: Sara?
S: Yes?
E: Is Jim's birthday in December?
S: December? No, it isn't. It's in February.
E: How old is he this year? Is he 50?
S: No, he's 49.
E: OK. And Rory's birthday is in March.
S: Yes.
E: What about Matt?
S: Matt's birthday is in June.
E: Are you sure?
S: Yes.
E: And when's your sister's birthday? July?
S: Eve? No, her birthday's in August. And she's 21!
E: Oh yes! Oh, and Kate and Paul. It's their wedding anniversary in November. That's it.
S: What about December?
E: What about it?
S: It's our wedding anniversary.
E: Oh yes! Of course.

1.46
January   May   September
February   June   October
March   July   November
April   August   December

1.47
1 young   3 old   5 small
2 rich   4 big   6 poor

1.48
1 **A:** Where are Paul and Jen today?
  B: They're at a wedding. The bride is Jen's sister.
2 **A:** Is Jack in the office this week?
  B: No, he's at a meeting in Paris.
3 **A:** Where are you?
  B: We're at home. My parents are here.

1.50
A: Congratulations!
B: Thank you. We're very happy.
A: Ah, she's lovely. What's her name?
B: It's Juba.
A: Hello, Juba.

1.51
1 **A:** Emma and I are engaged.
  B: Wow! Congratulations!
  A: Thanks very much.
  B: I'm very happy for you. When's the wedding?
  A: We're not sure … maybe in August.
2 **C:** Hello!
  D: Hello, come in.
  C: Happy Anniversary!
  D: Oh, thanks!
  C: How many years is it?
  D: Twenty-five.
  C: Wow! Twenty-five years.
3 **E:** Happy Birthday, Freya!
  F: Thank you.
  E: How old are you? Nineteen or twenty?
  F: Actually, I'm twenty-one.
  E: Oh, great!

1.53
C: Hello, Elena. It's nice to see you.
E: Hi, Celia. This is for the baby.
C: Oh, that's very kind.
E: You're welcome.
C: Well, thank you very much.
E: Now, where *is* the baby?
C: She's with my mother. Follow me.

Unit 4

1.55
Shanghai is a city in China. Shanghai is big, but it isn't the capital city – Beijing is the capital of China. Shanghai is a rich city. A lot of the buildings in Shanghai are new. The Pearl TV tower is in Shanghai. It's famous in China. Tourists from around the world visit Shanghai. They visit the river and the Pearl TV tower.

1.56
1 a park
2 a car park
3 a café
4 a market
5 an information centre
6 a bus station
7 a train station
8 a bank
9 a museum
10 a cinema

1.57
1 **A:** Excuse me?
  B: Yes?
  A: Where's the train station?
  B: It's in Exeter Street.
  A: Is it near here?
  B: Yes, it is.
  A: OK. Thanks.
2 **C:** Excuse me?
  D: Yes?
  C: Is the information centre near here?
  D: Yes, it is. It's near the park.
  C: OK. Thanks.
3 **E:** Excuse me?
  F: Yes?
  E: Is the car park in this street?
  F: No, it isn't. This is Exeter Street. The car park's in Oxford Street. It's next to the park.
  E: Thank you very much.
4 **G:** Excuse me?
  H: Yes?
  G: Where's the bank?
  H: I'm not sure. Oh! It's opposite the museum.
  G: Is it near here?
  H: Yes, it is.
  G: OK. Thanks.

1.58
T: Hi.
A: Good morning.
T: Is this a map of the city?
A: No, it isn't. That's a map of the city.
T: OK. And where's Big Ben?
A: It's near the River Thames … here it is.
T: Oh yes. Is it open on Sunday?
A: No, it isn't. It isn't open to tourists.

1.59
1 **A:** Excuse me. Is that a map of London?
  B: Yes, it is.
2 **A:** Is this a train timetable?
  B: No, it's a bus timetable.
3 **A:** Is that guidebook in English?
  B: Where?
  A: The book next to you.
  B: No, it isn't. It's in Spanish.

1.60
1 Monday   5 Friday
2 Tuesday   6 Saturday
3 Wednesday   7 Sunday
4 Thursday

1.61
T: Are museums open on Monday?
A: Yes, they're. They're open every day of the week.
T: OK. Are shops open every day?
A: Yes, they are. They're open every day of the week too.
T: Are banks open on Sunday?
A: No, they aren't. They're open Monday to Friday in the morning and afternoon. And they're open on Saturday morning.

1.62
a It's eleven o'clock.
b It's nine thirty.
c It's four fifteen.
d It's seven forty-five.
e It's eight twenty.
f It's three fifty-five.

🎵 1.63

1 Q: What time is it?
  A: It's five o'clock.
2 Q: What time is it?
  A: It's one thirty.
3 Q: What time is it?
  A: It's seven fifteen.
4 Q: What time is it?
  A: It's nine forty-five.
5 Q: What time is it?
  A: It's two twenty.
6 Q: What time is it?
  A: It's six o'clock.

🎵 1.64

1 mineral water   5 salad
2 fruit juice   6 tea
3 cake   7 sandwich
4 coffee

🎵 1.65

1 A: Hi. Can I help you?
  C: Two coffees, please.
  A: Large or small?
  C: Small.
  A: Anything else?
  C: No, thanks.
2 A: Hi. Can I help you?
  C: Can I have a mineral water, please?
  A: Anything else?
  C: Yes. A salad.
  A: OK. Four pounds, please.
3 A: Can I help you?
  C: A tea and a fruit juice, please
  A: Anything else?
  C: Yes. Two cakes, please.
  A: OK. Here you are. Seven pounds, please.
  C: Here you are.

Unit 5

🎵 1.68

Look at this fantastic photo. It's not a toy or a robot – this is a man. His name's Yves Rossy – or *Jetman* – and he can fly. Rossy is from Switzerland. Here, Rossy is above the Swiss Alps. He's in the air for a short time – only five minutes. But it's fantastic!

🎵 1.69

1 Robots can speak.
2 Robots can carry things.
3 People can't fly.
4 I can speak English.
5 My grandfather can't run.

🎵 1.71

L: Hi. Welcome to 'Technology Today'. I'm Lewis Jones and this morning I'm in a university technology department. I'm here with Christine Black and Tomo, a Japanese robot. Hi, Christine.
C: Hi, Lewis.
L: Christine, tell me about this robot.
C: Well, Tomo is from Japan. She's from a new generation of robots. They can do things that people can do.
L: 'She'? Or 'it'?
C: Aha! We say 'she'. She's a robot.
L: OK. So, she's from Japan. Can she speak Japanese?
C: Oh yes, she can speak Japanese and English.

L: OK. Can she sing?
C: Yes, she can.
L: And can she play the piano?
C: Yes, she can.
L: Wow! I can't sing or play the piano. Can she swim?
C: Well, Tomo can't swim, but some robots can swim.
L: OK. Well, my last question is about the name. What does 'Tomo' mean?
C: It means 'intelligent' in Japanese.
L: OK, Christine, thanks very much.
C: Thanks!

🎵 1.72

1 This laptop has a webcam.
2 This laptop has headphones.
3 This mobile phone has a camera.
4 This mobile phone has a video camera.
5 This mobile phone has an MP3 player.

🎵 1.73

a two pounds thirty
b thirteen pounds fifty
c fifteen euros
d three euros seventy-five
e seventeen dollars eighty
f eighteen dollars

🎵 1.74

1 It's thirty pounds.
2 It's forty pounds.
3 It's fifteen pounds.
4 It's sixteen pounds.
5 It's seventy pounds.
6 It's eighteen pounds.

🎵 1.75

1 A: Can I help you?
  C: How much is this alarm clock?
  A: This is a clock radio. It's fifty pounds.
  C: Hmm, that's a bit expensive. Thanks.
  A: That's OK. No problem.
2 A: Can I help you?
  C: Yes, I'd like this video camera, please.
  A: Certainly.
  C: Is it HD?
  A: Yes, it is. The image quality is fantastic.
  C: Great.
  A: OK, that's ninety-five pounds fifty, please.
  C: Here you are.
3 C: Excuse me.
  A: Yes, can I help you?
  C: How much are these memory sticks?
  A: They're five ninety-nine each.
  C: Can I pay with euros?
  A: Yes, of course.

Unit 6

🎵 1.77

These fans are passionate about football. Their team is the Kaizer Chiefs. Football and rugby are big sports in South Africa today. Football is an international sport – about 270 million people play football in more than 200 countries. The football World Cup is every four years. The World Cup prize is millions of dollars – $30 million at the World Cup in South Africa! Many international football players are millionaires. Football is a sport of passion and money!

🎵 1.78

1 I like my garden.
2 I don't like competitions.
3 My friends like sports.
4 I don't like football.
5 We like tennis.

🎵 1.79

cheese	fruit	salad
chocolate	meat	vegetables
eggs	pasta	
fish	rice	

🎵 1.80

I: Hi, Steve. Congratulations on your prize.
S: Thank you very much.
I: So, you are passionate about vegetables. But do you like fruit?
S: Yes, I do. I like fruit. I have a lot of fruit in my garden.
I: We know you don't like pumpkin pie. Do you like fruit pie?
S: No, I don't. But people in my family like fruit pie a lot.
I: So, giant vegetables are very important to you. But what about other food? What do you like?
S: Oh well, I like salad.
I: Do you like meat?
S: No, I don't – but I like fish.
I: And pasta? Do you like pasta?
S: Yes, I do. I like spaghetti and I like macaroni too.
I: OK, thanks very much, Steve.
S: Thank you!

🎵 1.82

Birds and fish are animals.
Detective stories and novels are books.
Action films and comedies are films.
Jazz and pop are types of music.
Scuba diving and swimming are sports.
Reality shows and wildlife shows are TV shows.

🎵 1.83

1 He likes fish.
2 He likes Botswana.
3 He doesn't like cold places.
4 He likes water.
5 He likes coffee.

🎵 1.84

1 A: Let's watch TV tonight.
  B: That's a good idea. What's on?
  A: A film with Emily Blunt is on at eight o'clock.
  B: Oh, I love her. She's fantastic.
2 C: Let's play table tennis tomorrow.
  D: No, thanks. I don't like table tennis.
  C: OK. How about football?
  D: Sorry. Sport's boring.
3 E: Let's have pasta this weekend.
  F: I don't like pasta. It's horrible.
  E: OK. How about pizza? Do you like pizza?
  F: Yes, it's great.

🎵 1.85

She's fantastic.	It's horrible.
Sport's boring.	It's great.

Unit 7

2.1

The Holi festival – or Festival of colours – is in March. It's a very happy festival. It's a celebration of spring and new life. People say 'goodbye' to winter and 'hello' to spring. In India, the winter months are December, January and February. The Holi festival is one or two days. It's a big celebration in parts of India and in other parts of the world.

2.3

The traditional Sami understand reindeer. In summer, they live in traditional tents. They have tractors. Today many young Sami live in modern homes. They have television and the Internet. They don't understand traditional Sami life.

2.4

They don't understand traditional Sami life.
They don't live in France.
We don't study Sami.
I don't have a car.

2.5

I: Hello, Miriam. Nice to meet you.
M: Hello.
I: Do you work at Kakenya's school?
M: Yes, I do. I teach there. We have five teachers.
I: Do you like it?
M: Yes, I do.
I: Do boys study at the school?
M: No, they don't. The school is for girls.
I: Only girls?
M: Yes, only girls.
I: That's unusual!
M: Yes, it is.
I: Do the girls live with their families?
M: No, they don't. They live at the school.
I: OK. And do they go home in summer?
M: Yes, they do. They go home to their villages.
I: Do the girls learn English at the school?
M: Yes, they do. And in summer we teach extra classes in English too.
I: OK. Thank you, Miriam.
M: Thank you.

2.6

I: Hi, Carl.
C: Hi.
I: Do you study at a college?
C: No, I don't. I'm at university.
I: Do you have classes every day?
C: No, I don't. I have classes on Monday, Wednesday, Thursday and Friday.
I: Do you like your classes?
C: Yes, I do.
I: Do you live near your university?
C: Yes, I do.
I: Do you live with your family?
C: No, I don't. I live with an English family.
I: Do you go home in the holidays?
C: Yes, I do. I go home in summer and in December.

2.7

1 Do you study at a college?
2 Do you have classes every day?
3 Do you like your classes?
4 Do you live near your university?
5 Do you live with your family?
6 Do you go home in the holidays?

2.9

1 I live in Canada. My favourite time of year is winter. It's cold and snowy.
2 I live in South Africa. I like spring. It's sunny and it isn't cold.
3 I live in the north of Australia. Summer is the wet season. It's hot and rainy. I don't like it!
4 I live in Great Britain. In autumn here, it's cloudy. It's windy too, but I like it. We don't have a dry season!

2.10

1 Ooh, I'm cold.
2 I'm tired.
3 I'm thirsty.
4 Uff, I'm hot.
5 Ugh, I'm wet.
6 Oh, I'm bored.
7 Mmm, I'm hungry.

2.11

a I'm bored.
b I'm cold.
c I'm hot.
d I'm hungry.
e I'm thirsty.
f I'm tired.
g I'm wet.

2.12

M: What's the matter?
F: It's cold and I'm thirsty.
M: Why don't you have a cup of tea? Here you are.
F: Thanks.
M: Paul, are you OK?
P: No, I'm not. I don't feel well.
M: Why don't you eat a sandwich? Here.
P: No, thanks. I'm not hungry. I'm cold and I'm wet.
M: What's the matter, Anna?
A: I'm bored.
M: Why don't you go to the beach? Go swimming.
A: In the rain?!? Mum!
M: I don't understand you all. We're on holiday!

2.13

Why don't you have a cup of tea?
I don't feel well.
I don't understand you all.

Unit 8

2.15

I: Do you like your job?
M: Yes, I love my job. I'm a farmer. I don't work in an office. I work outside. I work in Nevada, in the United States. Every day is different in my job.
I: What do you do?
M: We work with animals. Today farmers use modern technology. We have mobile phones and computers. We don't use tractors – we use helicopters!

2.16

1 I get up at six o'clock.
2 I have breakfast at six thirty.
3 I start work at seven o'clock.
4 I have lunch in a café.
5 I finish work at five forty-five.
6 I have dinner at home.
7 I go to bed at eleven thirty.

2.17

Chen Hong is from Shanghai. She's a writer. She gets up at six o'clock in the morning. She doesn't have breakfast. She goes to an exercise class. The class is on the Bund, near the river. It starts at seven o'clock and it finishes at 7.45. Then Chen has breakfast with her friends. She starts work at 9.30. She works at home. At midday, she has lunch. She finishes work at 6.15 in the evening. At eight o'clock, she has dinner with her friends. She goes to bed at 10.30. Chen Hong doesn't work every day, but she goes to her exercise class every day.

2.18

1 He works in Chile.
2 He starts work at nine o'clock.
3 He finishes work at 1.30.
4 He goes to bed at two o'clock.
5 He gets up at 8.45.

2.19

M: Who's Cynthia Liutkus-Pierce? Does she work at this university?
W: Yes, she does.
M: I don't know her. Does she teach languages?
W: No, she doesn't.
M: What does she do?
W: She's a geologist.
M: Oh, OK. Does she give lectures?
W: Yes, she does. And she works in Africa.
M: Oh, does she go to Africa every year?
W: Yes, she does. She goes in summer.
M: I know some geologists in Africa. Where does Cynthia go?
W: I don't know. I think she goes to Tanzania.
M: Oh, my friends are in Angola.

2.20

1 R: Good morning, PJ International. Can I help you?
C: Yes, can I speak to Ed Carr, please?
R: I'm sorry. He's in a meeting.
C: OK, thank you. I'll call back later. Goodbye.
R: Goodbye.
2 R: Hello, Green Wildlife Park. Can I help you?
C: Good morning. Can I speak to Mr Watts, please?
R: Yes, one moment, please.
C: Thank you.
3 R: Good morning, City College. Can I help you?
C: Yes, can I speak to Mrs Jackson, please?
R: I'm sorry. She's out of the office at the moment.
C: OK, thank you. I'll call back later. Goodbye.
R: Goodbye.

Unit 9

2.24

1 I travel from Paris to London for my job. I go every week. I usually go by train because I can work on the train.
2 I'm an Australian student and I travel in my holidays. I love Asia! I travel by bus. It's really interesting. You meet a lot of people.
3 I live in San Francisco. I don't like flying, so I never travel by plane. I don't really travel.
4 I'm from Madrid, but my parents live in Mallorca. I visit them every summer. I usually go by boat.

🎵 2.26

There's a camera.
There's a laptop.
There are three scarves.
There are two shirts.
There's a pair of shoes.
There's a skirt.
There are some T-shirts.

🎵 2.28

S: OK, that's the flight. Let's look for a hotel now. Is it for two nights or three?
L: Three nights – Friday, Saturday and Sunday. Are there any hotels near the airport?
S: Yes, there are. But they're expensive. Just a minute … no, there aren't any cheap hotels near the airport. They're all expensive. This one is four hundred dollars a night!
L: Wow! Well, what about a youth hostel? Is there a youth hostel near the airport?
S: OK, let's see. I don't think so … no, there isn't. I don't like youth hostels. They aren't very comfortable.
L: OK. Let's look in the city centre. Are there any cheap hotels there?
S: Yes, of course there are.
L: Well, that's good. And is there a bus to the city centre?
S: A bus from the airport? Yes, there is. There's a bus every twenty minutes from the airport to the centre. There isn't a train, but that's OK.
L: And there are taxis too.
S: I think the bus is fine. OK, so let's look at these hotels.

🎵 2.29

1	TV	5 table	9 wardrobe
2	bath	6 lamp	10 armchair
3	bed	7 desk	11 shower
4	chair	8 sofa	12 fridge

🎵 2.30

L: Wow, this room is really big! Oh, it's two rooms! The bed is in here, look!
S: It's fantastic!
L: I know. And it isn't really expensive …
S: Are you sure?
L: Yes. Oh, I like these lamps!
S: Yes, they're really unusual!
L: This sofa is very comfortable. And what's this? Oh, it's a fridge.
S: Are there any drinks in it? I'm really thirsty.
L: Yes, there are some bottles of water. Here.
S: Thanks.
S: Where's the TV?
L: I don't know. There isn't one.
S: What? There isn't a TV!

🎵 2.31

R: Good afternoon, sir. Can I help you?
G: Hello. Yes, I'd like an alarm call at 7.30, please.
R: In the morning? Certainly, sir. What's your room number?
G: 327.
R: OK, 327 … an alarm call for 7.30.
G: And I'd like to have a meal in my room this evening.
R: Of course. There's a menu in your room. It's on the desk.
G: Oh, yes!
R: Call 101 for room service.
G: Fine. I'd like to use the Internet too.

R: No problem, sir. There's wi-fi in all the rooms.
G: Great. Oh, and is there a bank near the hotel?
R: Yes, there's one in this street. It's next to the cinema.
G: OK, thanks very much.

🎵 2.32

I'd like an alarm call at 7.30, please.
I'd like to have a meal in my room.
I'd like to use the Internet too.

Unit 10

🎵 2.34

This photo shows an important moment in television history. The two men are in a laboratory in New Jersey, in the United States. There are four televisions in the photo. Television A has a red picture, television B has a green picture and television C has a blue picture. But the picture on the television next to the man is in full colour. The year is 1950 and the photo shows the tests on a new invention – colour television.

🎵 2.36

1950 colour television
1963 video recorders
1973 mobile phones
1975 digital cameras
1993 MP3 players
1995 digital television
2006 Blu-ray discs

🎵 2.37

The first round-the-world expedition was from 1519 to 1522. The expedition captain was Ferdinand Magellan.

The first successful South Pole expedition was in 1911. The expedition leader was Roald Amundsen.

The first man in space was Yuri Gagarin. The first woman in space was Valentina Tereshkova. They were both from Russia.

On 16 May 1975, Junko Tabei was the first woman at the top of Everest.

The first woman at the North Pole was Ann Bancroft on 1 May 1986.

🎵 2.39

He was born in 1480.
He was an explorer.
He was Portuguese.
They were explorers.
They were from Russia.

🎵 2.40

first	eighth	fifteenth
second	ninth	sixteenth
third	tenth	seventeenth
fourth	eleventh	eighteenth
fifth	twelfth	nineteenth
sixth	thirteenth	twentieth
seventh	fourteenth	

🎵 2.42

the first of May 1986
the second of June 1953
the third of November 1957
the fourth of October 1957
the twelfth of April 1961
the thirteenth of December 1972
the fourteenth of December 1911
the sixteenth of May 1975
the twentieth of July 1969

🎵 2.43

I: Aneta, who was your hero when you were young?
A: When I was about ten years old, my hero was Michael Johnson. He was a great sportsman.
I: Was he the Olympic champion?
A: Yes, he was. And he was the world champion eight times.
I: Were you good at sports at school?
A: Well … yes, I was. I was in the basketball team at school.
I: Joe, who was your hero when you were young?
J: When I was young, my hero was David Attenborough. He was on television. His programmes about animals and nature were fantastic.
I: Was it his first job?
J: No, it wasn't. His first job was with books, but he wasn't happy in that job.
I: Which is your favourite David Attenborough programme?
J: I think it's *Life on Earth*. But all his programmes were really interesting.
I: That was in 1979 … were you born then?
J: No, I wasn't! But I have the DVD.
I: Clare, who was your hero when you were young?
C: My heroes weren't famous. They were my teachers at college. I wasn't happy at school, but college was great. The teachers were really nice and friendly. Mrs Harvey was my art teacher. She was very funny. And she was married to my English teacher, Mr Harvey.
I: Were they good teachers?
C: Yes, they were. They were fantastic.

🎵 2.45

1 **T:** Hello!
   S: Hi, I'm sorry I'm late. The bus was late.
   T: That's OK. Take a seat.
2 **C:** Oh, hi Ravi.
   R: Hi Clare.
   C: Erm, the meeting was at 2.30. Where were you?
   R: Oh, I'm sorry. I was very busy.
   C: It's OK. It wasn't an important meeting.
3 **A:** Mmm, this coffee is good!
   B: Yes, it is.
   A: So, what about yesterday? We were at your house at ten o'clock. Where were you?
   B: I'm very sorry. We weren't at home. We were at my sister's house!
   A: It's OK. Don't worry.

🎵 2.46

1 I'm <u>sorry</u> I'm late.
2 The <u>bus</u> was late.
3 I was very <u>busy</u>.
4 We <u>weren't</u> at <u>home</u>.

Unit 11

🎵 2.48

Scientists discover hundreds of new plants and animals every year. A large number of these discoveries are in Indonesia. In fact, scientists in Papua New Guinea usually find about two new plants or animals every week. It's a fantastic place. There aren't many people in the area and it isn't easy to get there. Scientists sometimes arrive and leave by helicopter!

🎵 2.49

The scientists at the University of Innsbruck started their investigation. They took photos and they studied the body. They discovered the body was a man. They called him 'Ötzi' because the body was in the Ötztal mountains in the Alps. The scientists finished their report. It was very interesting.

Ötzi was a small man. He was about 45 years old when he died. He was from the north of Italy and he lived about 5,000 years ago. The scientists think he walked to the mountains. The scientists think he died in spring. They also think an arrow killed him.

🎵 2.51

I: Hi, Jamie.

J: Hello.

I: Did you watch Alastair's videos?

J: Well, I didn't see the first or second video, but I saw a video about swimming in the River Thames.

I: Did you like it?

J: Yes, I did. I liked it a lot. The next weekend, I didn't stay at home. I drove to a lake near my house and went swimming.

I: Was that an adventure?

J: Yes, because usually I go to the swimming pool. It was very different in the lake.

I: Did you make a video too?

J: Yes, my friend went with me. He filmed me on his camera phone and we sent the video to Alastair on Twitter.

🎵 2.53

1 A: Did you and Sonia have a good time in Sydney last week?

B: Yes, thanks, we did. But we didn't go swimming.

A: Oh? Why not?

B: There was a shark in the sea!

2 C: Did you and Jack have a good holiday last year?

D: No, we didn't.

C: Oh? Why not?

D: Well, we stayed at home. We didn't have any money!

3 E: Did you and Alice have a nice meal last night?

F: Yes, we did. It was delicious. And we didn't pay!

E: Oh? Why not?

F: My boss paid!

🎵 2.54

We didn't go swimming.
We didn't have any money.
We didn't pay!

Unit 12

🎵 2.56

The young women in this photo work in a factory from Monday to Saturday. But today is Sunday – it's the weekend. On Sunday, they usually meet and go out for the day. Most shops, museums and cinemas are open, so there are a lot of things to do. In different countries, the weekend is on different days. In some countries – for example, Oman – the weekend is Thursday and Friday. In Algeria, Egypt and Qatar, the weekend is Friday and Saturday. These Chinese factory workers have one day off, but office workers have Saturday off too. The Saturday and Sunday weekend is quite new in China – it started in 1995.

🎵 2.57

1	a fridge, an oven	kitchen
2	a chair, a table	dining room
3	an armchair, a sofa	living room
4	a bed, a wardrobe	bedroom
5	a bath, a shower, a toilet	bathroom

🎵 2.59

I: Ayu, tell us about these photos.

A: Well, this is my mother. She's in the kitchen. She's cooking.

I: What's she making?

A: She's making lunch. We have a big family lunch every Saturday.

I: And who's this?

A: That's my husband, Amir, in the bathroom. He's bathing our daughter.

I: How old is your daughter?

A: She's eighteen months old. And this is my father with his friend. They're talking and drinking coffee.

I: What are they sitting on?

A: They're sitting on the mats we use in Indonesia. And then this photo is Amir's brother with his son.

I: What are they doing? Are they reading?

A: No, they aren't. They're playing a game on Amir's computer. This is my sister. She's in the bedroom. She's ironing. I usually help her.

I: And what about this last one?

A: This is my brother – he's wearing an orange T-shirt – and his friend. They're washing their motorbikes. They do that every Saturday.

I: Which is your favourite photo?

A: Oh, I think it's the one of my husband and my daughter because they are both smiling and happy.

🎵 2.60

A: Hi Lauren, it's Alex.

L: Oh, hello. Where are you?

A: I'm on the bus. I'm going home from work. So, what are you doing this weekend?

L: Well, I'm going shopping tomorrow.

A: Of course. You always go shopping on Saturdays.

L: No, I don't! Anyway, Sports Gear is having a sale tomorrow.

A: Really?

L: Yes, they're selling all the winter sports stuff at half price.

A: Wow! And what about on Sunday?

L: I don't know. What are you doing?

A: Well, do you remember Helen Skelton? She went down the Amazon River last year.

L: Oh yes.

A: She's giving a talk about her trip on Sunday evening. I'm going with my brother. Would you like to come?

L: Where is it?

A: At the Natural Science Museum. Tickets are free.

L: OK! Why not?

🎵 2.62

A: What are you doing this weekend?

O: I'm not sure. My sister is coming tomorrow.

A: Is she staying the weekend?

O: Yes, she is. We're going to a party on Saturday.

A: Does she like music? The West Country Folk Band is playing at the City Hall on Sunday.

O: OK. Great!

🎵 2.63

a C: Four tickets for the museum, please.

S: Four adults?

C: Oh sorry, no. Two adults and two children.

S: OK. That's six pounds, please. Would you like a brochure for the *Home Life* exhibition?

C: Yes, please.

S: Would you like it in English? We have brochures in French, German and Japanese too.

C: Oh, French, please.

S: Here you are.

C: Thanks.

b C: Three return tickets to Lindisfarne, please.

S: Are you coming back today?

C: Yes, we are. Is there a bus after six o'clock?

S: Yes, there is. There's a bus every hour. The last one is at nine o'clock.

C: OK.

S: Are you going to the castle and gardens? Would you like to buy the tickets now?

C: Oh, yes. Great.

S: It's a special weekend ticket. That's twenty-one pounds, please.

C: Here you are.

S: Thank you.

c S: Good morning.

C: Hi. It's busy today! Are there any free tennis courts?

S: Yes, there are. The people on court 4 are finishing now.

C: OK, great. A ticket for two people, please.

S: Would you like it for one hour or two hours?

C: Erm, just a minute … Ellen, would you like to play for one hour or two?

E: One is fine.

C: OK. So just one hour, please.

S: That's ten pounds.

C: Thanks.

🎵 2.64

Would you like a brochure for the *Home Life* exhibition?

Would you like it in English?

Would you like to buy the tickets now?

NATIONAL GEOGRAPHIC
L E A R N I N G

Life Beginner Student's Book

Helen Stephenson, Paul Dummett and John Hughes

Publisher: Gavin McLean

Publishing Consultant: Karen Spiller

Editorial Project Manager: Karen Spiller

Development Editor: Liz Driscoll

Development Editor (DVD): Jennifer Nunan

Strategic Marketing Manager: Charlotte Ellis

Project Editor: Amy Borthwick

Production Controller: Elaine Willis

Art Director: Natasa Arsenidou

Cover Designers: Sofia Fourtouni
    and Vasiliki Christoforidou

Text Designer: Keith Shaw

Compositor: emc design ltd

National Geographic Liaison: Leila Hishmeh

Audio: Prolingua Productions

DVD: Tom, Dick and Debbie Ltd

The publishers would like to thank the following for their advisory role in the preparation of this material: Lobat Asadi (Middle East) and Sharon Bromwich (Teacher, Australia language school).

For product information and technology assistance, contact us at
Cengage Learning Customer & Sales Support, cengage.com/contact

For permission to use material from this text or product,
submit all requests online at **cengage.com/permissions**
Further permissions questions can be emailed to
permissionrequest@cengage.com

ISBN: 978-1-133-31568-1

National Geographic Learning
Cheriton House, North Way, Andover, Hampshire, SP10 5BE
United Kingdom

National Geographic Learning, a Cengage Learning Company, has a mission to bring the world to the classroom and the classroom to life. With our English language programs, students learn about their world by experiencing it. Through our partnerships with National Geographic and TED Talks, they develop the language and skills they need to be successful global citizens and leaders.

Locate your local office at **international.cengage.com/region**

Visit National Geographic Learning online at **NGL.Cengage.com/ELT**
Visit our corporate website at **www.cengage.com**

CREDITS
Although every effort has been made to contact copyright holders before publication, this has not always been possible. If contacted, the publisher will undertake to rectify any errors or omissions at the earliest opportunity.

The publishers would like to thank the following sources for permission to reproduce their copyright protected images and videos:
Cover photo: Paul Nicklen/National Geographic Image Collection
Inside photos: pp 6 tl (Mike Theiss/National Geographic Image Collection), 6 mr (Mr Standfast/Alamy), 6 bl (DreamPictures/Photographer's Choice/Getty Images), 7 tl (Eric Chretien/Contributor/Gamma-Rapho/Getty Images), 7 mr (Alex Treadway/National Geographic Image Collection), 7 bl (Michael Nichols/ National Geographic Image Collection), 8 tl (David Doubilet/National Geographic Image Collection), 8 tm (Richard Nowitz/National Geographic Image Collection), 8 tr (Carla Dedominicis/National Geographic My Shot), 8 ul (Justin Guariglia/National Geographic Image Collection), 8 um (Laurent Gillieron/AFP/ Getty Images), 8 ur (Gallo Images/Getty Images), 8 ll (Dibyangshu Sarkar/Stringer/AFP/Getty Images), 8 lm (Melissa Farlow/National Geographic Image Collection), 8 lr (Michael S. Lewis/National Geographic Image Collection), 8 bl (Willard Culver/National Geographic Image Collection), 8 bm (Tim Laman/ National Geographic Image Collection), 8 br (Cary Wolinsky/National Geographic Image Collection), 9 (David Doubilet/National Geographic Image Collection), 10 m (Monika Klum/National Geographic Image Collection), 10 bfl (Mark Thiessen/National Geographic Image Collection), 10 bml (O. Louis Mazzatenta/ National Geographic Image Collection), 10 bmr (Mark Thiessen/National Geographic Image Collection), 10 bfr (Alex Treadway), 11 1 (Jose Elias/Lusoimages – Technology/Alamy), 11 2 (medical images/Alamy), 11 3 (Ryan McVay/Photodisc/Getty Images), 11 4 (Gino's Premium Images/Alamy), 11 5 (Nikreates/Alamy), 11 6 (ilian return/Alamy), 12 ml (Alex Treadway/National Geographic Image Collection), 12 bl (Alex Treadway/National Geographic Image Collection), 13 a (amana images inc./Alamy), 13 b (Shutterstock), 13 c (Larry Lilac/Alamy), 13 d (Blend Images/Alamy), 13 quick quiz 01 (David Gee 1/Alamy), 13 quick quiz 02 (foodfolio/ Alamy), 13 quick quiz 03 (Sean Nel/Alamy), 13 quick quiz 04 (LOOK Die Bildagentur der Fotografen GmbH/Alamy), 15 Anne-Marie Blanc (Andres Rodriguez/ Alamy), 15 Juan Garcia (Custom Medical Stock Photo/Alamy), 15 Nelson Pires (LatinStock Collection/Alamy), 15 Naomi Smith (RubberBall/Alamy), 16 tl (Shutterstock), 16 tr (PhotoAlto/Alamy), 18 (Alex Treadway/National Geographic Image Collection), 19 (Shutterstock), 20 1 (Shutterstock), 20 2 (Ian Miles– Flashpoint Pictures/Alamy), 20 3 (Shutterstock), 20 4 (Shutterstock), 20 5 (Shutterstock), 20 6 (Shutterstock), 21 (Richard Nowitz/National Geographic Image Collection), 22 (Tim Hall/Stockbyte/Getty Images), 23 (Simeone Huber/Photographer's Choice/Getty Images), 24 (Aurora Photos/Alamy), 25 (Corbis Cusp/ Alamy), 26 (Bruno Schlumberger/National Geographic My Shot), 27 (Mauro Ladu/Alamy), 27 (Peter Adams/Digital Vision/Getty Images), 27 (Annie Griffiths/ National Geographic Image Collection), 27 (Dmitri Alexander/National Geographic Image Collection), 28 tl (Chris Howes/Wild Places Photography/Alamy), 28 ml (vario images GmbH & Co.KG/Alamy), 29 tl (Blend Images/Alamy), 29 bl (Aki/Alamy), 30 (DreamPictures/Photographer's Choice/Getty Images), 31 (Planetobserver/Science Photo Library), 32 (Shutterstock), 33 (Carla Dedominicis/National Geographic My Shot), 34 (Keenpress/National Geographic Image Collection), 35 (Gordon Wiltsie/National Geographic Image Collection), 37 (christian kober/Alamy), 39 (AAD Worldwide Travel Images/Alamy), 39 (Karen Kasmauski/Corbis), 40 (Kuttig – Travel – 2/Alamy), 42 (Lynn Johnson/National Geographic Image Collection), 43 ur (Lynn Johnson/National Geographic Image Collection), 43 lr (Joel Sartore/National Geographic Image Collection), 44 (Kellie Netherwood), 45 (Justin Guariglia/National Geographic Image Collection), 46 1 (Shutterstock), 46 2 (Sami Sarkis (4)/Alamy), 46 3 (Fancy/Alamy), 46 4 (Dave Porter/Alamy), 46 5 (The Photolibrary Wales/Alamy), 46 6 (dbimages/Alamy), 46 7 (Randy Olson/National Geographic Image Collection), 46 8 (geodigital/Alamy), 46 9 (VIEW Pictures Ltd/Alamy), 46 10 (Ferenc Szelepcsenyi/Alamy), 46 lr (Bailey-Cooper Photography/Alamy), 46 br (Bailey-Cooper Photography/Alamy), 47 lr (Ian Dagnall/Alamy), 47 br (Anna Stowe Botanica/Alamy),

Printed in China by RR Donnelley
Print Number: 06   Print Year: 2017

48 (incamerastock/Alamy), 49 tl (Gianluca Colla/National Geographic Image Collection), 49 tr (Carolyn Clarke/Alamy), 50 (Bruce Dale/National Geographic Image Collection), 51 (Carole Anne Ferris/Alamy), 52 tl (Rhys Stacker/Alamy), 52 a (Bon Appetit/Alamy), 52 b (Nikreates/Alamy), 52 c (Lucie Lang/Alamy), 52 d (Shutterstock), 52 e (David Lee/Alamy), 52 f (Lenscap/Alamy), 52 g (whiteboxmedia limited/Alamy), 53 (Dennis Cox/Alamy), 54 (Mike Theiss/National Geographic Image Collection), 57 (Laurent Gillieron/AFP/Getty Images), 58 (Randy Olson/National Geographic Image Collection), 59 1 (Bon Appetit/Alamy), 59 2 (Digital Vision/Getty Images), 59 3 (Aflo Foto Agency/Alamy), 59 4 (i love images/couples/Alamy), 59 5 (Shutterstock), 59 6 (Corbis Bridge/Alamy), 59 7 (FirstShot/Alamy), 59 8 (Image Source/Alamy), 59 bl (Yoshikazu Tsuno/AFP/Getty), 60 tl (Ron Bedard/Alamy), 60 tm (Vincenzo Lombardo/Photographer's Choice RF/Getty Images), 61 (Martin Benik/Alamy), 62 1 (A. T. Willett/Alamy), 62 2 (Shutterstock), 62 3 (Ingrid Balabanova/Alamy), 63 bl (Picture Contact BV/Alamy), 63 r (all Rebecca Hale/National Geographic Image Collection), 64 tr (images/Alamy), 64 alarm clock (studiomode/Alamy), 64 memory sticks (Alison Thompson/Alamy), 64 speakers (photonic 7/Alamy), 64 video camera (Simon Belcher/Alamy), 64 digital camera (James Boardman/Alamy), 64 headphones (Metta foto/Alamy), 64 MP3 player (Art Directors & TRIP/Alamy), 64 webcam (Jinx Photography RF/Alamy), 65 inset (David Cook/blueshiftstudios/Alamy), 65 b (Corbis RF/Alamy), 66 (Kevork Djansezian/Getty Images), 67 camera (Shutterstock), 67 coffee machine (Shutterstock), 67 laptop (Shutterstock), 67 microwave (Shutterstock), 67 memory stick (Shutterstock), 67 mobile phone (Shutterstock), 68 tl (Shutterstock), 68 ml (Jeff Morgan 07/Alamy), 69 (Gallo Images/Getty Images), 70 (Boston Globe/Getty Images), 71 cheese (incamerastock/Alamy), 71 chocolate (Brian Jackson/Alamy), 71 eggs (foodfolio/Alamy), 71 fish (Westmacott/Alamy), 71 fruit (OnWhite/Alamy), 71 meat (Edd Westmacott/Alamy), 71 pasta (Helen Sessions/Alamy), 71 rice (foodfolio/Alamy), 71 salad (foodfolio/Alamy), 71 vegetables (blickwinkel/Alamy), 72 (Brant Allen), 73 bl (Zeb Hogan), 74 athletes (ZUMA Wire Service/Alamy), 74 motorbikes (PhotoKratky – Editorial/Alamy), 74 cars (speedpix/Alamy), 74 boats (Horizon International Images Limited/Alamy), 74 bikes (Jordan Weeks/Alamy), 75 t (Santisiri Thor/National Geographic My Shot), 75 m (Goran Tomasevic/ Reuters/Corbis), 75 b (Brendon Boyes/Alamy), 76 t (Fuse/Getty Images), 77 tl (White Teeth by Zadie Smith (Hamish Hamilton, 2000). Copyright © Zadie Smith, 2000), 77 tm (Lionsgate/The Kobal Collection), 77 tr (Universal/The Kobal Collection), 78 (Mr Standfast/Alamy), 79 tl (robfood/Alamy), 79 tm (Marco Secchi/Alamy), 79 tr (Rawdon Wyatt/Alamy), 80 tl (Brian J. Skerry/National Geographic Image Collection), 81 (Dibyangshu Sarkar/Stringer/ AFP/Getty Images), 82 a (Franz Aberham/Photographer's Choice/Getty Images), 82 b (Franz Aberham/Photographer's Choice/Getty Images), 83 ml (Outdoor-Archiv/Alamy), 84 (Philip Scott Andrews/National Geographic Image Collection), 85 br (Purestock/Alamy), 87 a (Radius Images/Alamy), 87 b (D. Hurst/Alamy), 87 c (Ian Cook/All Canada Photos/Getty Images), 87 d (Antony SOUTER/Alamy), 88 t (Peter Macdiarmid/Staff/Getty Images News/ Getty Images), 89 t (i love images/Fitness/Alamy), 89 b (Catchlight Visual Services/Alamy), 90 (Eric Chretien/Contributor/Gamma-Rapho/Getty Images), 92 r (imagebroker/Alamy), 93 (Melissa Farlow/National Geographic Image Collection), 94 b (Justin Guariglia/National Geographic Image Collection), 95 ml (Jim Richardson/National Geographic Image Collection), 96 1 (Ken Gillespie Photography/Alamy), 96 2 (Emory Kristof/National Geographic Image Collection), 96 Cynthia Liutkus-Pierce (Carol Liutkus), 96 Julia Mayo Torne (Alfredo Fernandez Valmayor), 97 journalist (Blend Images/Alamy), 97 waiter (Corbis RF Best/Alamy), 97 businesswoman (Fancy/Alamy), 97 nurse (Olaf Doering/Alamy), 97 receptionist (Jim Wileman/Alamy), 97 shop assistant (Image Source/Alamy), 98 a (mike lane/Alamy), 98 b (Rainer Martini/LOOK Die Bildagentur der Fotografen GmbH/Alamy), 98 c (John Giustina/ Taxi/Getty Images), 98 d (D. Hurst/Alamy), 99 t (Steve Winter/National Geographic Image Collection), 99 mr (Steve Winter/National Geographic Image Collection), 100 tm (David Hancock/Alamy), 100 tr (Nick Dolding/Digital Vision/Getty Images), 100 m (Shoosmith Snack Foood Collection/Alamy), 100 mr (imagebroker/Alamy), 100 bm (PCN Photography/Alamy), 100 br (David Hoare/Alamy), 101 r (Sherwin Crasto/Reuters/Corbis), 102 (Michael Nichols/ National Geographic Image Collection), 104 l (Cary Wolinsky/National Geographic Image Collection), 105 t (Michael S. Lewis/National Geographic Image Collection), 106 boots (Shutterstock), 106 hat (Shutterstock), 106 coat (Shutterstock), 106 sandals (Shutterstock), 106 jacket (Shutterstock), 106 T-shirt (Shutterstock), 106 skirt (Shutterstock), 106 jeans (Shutterstock), 106 dress (Shutterstock), 106 top (Shutterstock), 106 shirt (Shutterstock), 106 trousers (Shutterstock), 106 scarf (Shutterstock), 106 shorts (Shutterstock), 106 jumper (Shutterstock), 106 shoes (Shutterstock), 107 b (Aurora Photos/ Alamy), 108 tl (Jan Greune/LOOK/Getty Images), 108 tr (imagebroker/Alamy), 109 1 (RichardBakerHeathrow/Alamy), 109 2 (Rob Cousins/Alamy), 109 3 (Y. Levy/Alamy), 109 4 (Shutterstock), 109 5 (Ace Stock Limited/Alamy), 109 6 (Shutterstock), 109 7 (eStock Photo/Alamy), 109 8 (Peter Alvey/Alamy), 109 9 (UpperCut Images/Alamy), 109 10 (LOOK Die Bildagentur der Fotografen GmbH/Alamy), 109 11 (Guns4Hire/Alamy), 109 12 (Shutterstock), 109 a (numb/ Alamy), 109 b (Curtseyes/Alamy), 111 t (Aaron Huey/National Geographic Image Collection), 111 bfl (Aaron Huey/National Geographic Image Collection), 111 bl (Shutterstock), 111 br (Olivier Renck/Aurora/Getty Images), 111 bfr (ITAR-TASS Photo Agency/Alamy), 112 t (Larry Lilac/Alamy), 113 t (adam eastland/ Alamy), 113 bl (nobleIMAGES/Alamy), 113 br (CW Images/Alamy), 114 (Kenneth Garrett/National Geographic Image Collection), 116 ml (Ian Nolan/Alamy), 117 t (Willard Culver/National Geographic Image Collection), 118 t (Barry Bishop/National Geographic Image Collection), 118 Ferdinand Magellan (Ferdinand Magellan, Armet Portanell, Jose (1843–1911)/Private Collection/© Look and Learn/The Bridgeman Art Library), 118 Yuri Gagarin (Bettmann/Corbis), 118 Roald Amundsen (Classic Image/Alamy), 118 Junko Tabei (Press Association Images), 118 Ann Bancroft (Obed Zilwa/AP/Press Association Images), 118 Valentina Tereshkova (RIA Novosti/Alamy), 120 t (Trinity Mirror/Mirrorpix/Alamy), 120 bm (David Young-Wolff/Alamy), 120 br (PCN Photography/ Alamy), 122 George Washington (B Christopher/Alamy), 122 Tupac Amaru (Georgios Kollidas/Alamy), 122 Hillary Clinton (epa european pressphoto agency b.v./Alamy), 122 Pocahontas (Three Lions/Stringer/Hulton Royals Collection/Getty Images), 122 Simon Bolivar (Simon Bolivar (1783–1830) (chromolitho), ./Private Collection/Archives Charmet/The Bridgeman Art Library), 122 Robert E. Lee (Archive Pics/Alamy), 123 (U.S. Gov't Nat'l Archives/ National Geographic Image Collection), 124 a (Shutterstock), 124 b (Shutterstock), 124 c (Shutterstock), 124 d (Shutterstock), 124 e (Shutterstock), 124 f (Joel Sartore/National Geographic Image Collection), 125 mr (Nancy G Western Photography, Nancy Greifenhagen/Alamy), 126 (Everett Collection Historical/Alamy), 127 a (Shutterstock), 127 b (Shutterstock), 127 c (Shutterstock), 127 d (Shutterstock), 128 ml (Neville Styles/Alamy), 129 t (Tim Laman/ National Geographic Image Collection), 131 tl (Press Association Images), 131 t (Kenneth Garrett/National Geographic Image Collection), 131 mr (Kenneth Garrett/National Geographic Image Collection), 132 b (Alastair Humphreys), 135 t (Stephen Alvarez/National Geographic Image Collection), 135 bl (Stephen Alvarez/National Geographic Image Collection), 135 br (Stephen Alvarez/National Geographic Image Collection), 136 t (David Doubilet/ National Geographic Image Collection), 137 mr (UpperCut Images/Alamy), 138 (Shutterstock), 140 ml (Michael Melford/National Geographic Image Collection), 140 mr (Shutterstock), 141 t (Cary Wolinsky/National Geographic Image Collection), 142 tm (Greg Dale/National Geographic Image Collection), 142 tr (Greg Dale/National Geographic Image Collection), 142 ml (Greg Dale/National Geographic Image Collection), 142 mr (Greg Dale/National Geographic Image Collection), 142 bl (Greg Dale/National Geographic Image Collection), 142 br (Greg Dale/National Geographic Image Collection), 143 br (Greg Dale/National Geographic Image Collection), 144 b (Werner Dieterich/Photographer's Choice/Getty Images), 147 tr (Tyrone Turner/National Geographic Image Collection), 147 b (Tyrone Turner/National Geographic Image Collection), 148 t (Alistair Brydon/Alamy), 150 (John Warburton-Lee Photography/Alamy), 152 ml (Richard Nowitz/National Geographic Image Collection), 153 driver (Shutterstock), 153 artist (Shutterstock), 153 photographer (Shutterstock), 153 writer (Shutterstock), 153 wedding A (Randy Olson/National Geographic Image Collection), 153 wedding B (Melissa Farlow/National Geographic Image Collection), 153 hotel in Middle East (Cephas Picture Library/Alamy), 154 tl (Shutterstock), 154 tr (Stuart Freedman/In Pictures/Corbis), 154 easy cook microwave (Shutterstock), 154 professional chef microwave (Samsung), 155 marathon (ADS/Alamy), 155 golf tournament (epa european pressphoto agency b.v./Alamy), 155 tennis tournament (Michael Cole/Corbis), 155 Tour de France (epa european pressphoto agency b.v./Alamy), 155 Dakar Rally (Eduardo Mariano Rivero/Alamy), 156 tl (Shutterstock), 156 ml (Shutterstock), 156 bl (Shutterstock), 157 filmmaker (Shutterstock), 157 engineer (Shutterstock), 157 doctor (Shutterstock), 157 teacher (Corbis Super RF/Alamy), 157 wedding A (Randy Olson/National Geographic Image Collection), 157 wedding B (Melissa Farlow/National Geographic Image Collection), 157 Times Square in winter (Ira Block/National Geographic Image Collection), 158 tl (Shutterstock), 158 tr (Stuart Freedman/In Pictures/Corbis), 158 easy cook microwave (Shutterstock), 158 professional chef microwave (Samsung), 155 marathon (ADS/Alamy), 159 golf tournament (epa european pressphoto agency b.v./Alamy), 159 tennis tournament (Michael Cole/Corbis), 159 Tour de France (epa european pressphoto agency b.v./Alamy), 159 Dakar rally (Shutterstock), 160 tl (Shutterstock), 160 ml (Shutterstock), 160 bl (Shutterstock)

DVD photos: National Geographic Image Collection (Unit 1: Alex Treadway, Charles Meacham, James L. Stanfield, Michael Melford, James P. Blair, Brian Skerry, Jimmy Chin, David Carter, Chris Johns; Unit 4: Justin Guariglia, Tino Soriano, Krista Rossow, James A. Sugar, Mike Theiss, Gordon Esler, Will Van Overbeek; Unit 8: Michael Nichols); Shutterstock (Unit 1, male photographer)

DVD videos: National Geographic Video Collection (Units 2, 3, 7–12). Special thanks to Erika Larsen/Redux Pictures (Unit 7, The people of the reindeer) and Nick Nichols/Nathan Williamson (Unit 8, The elephants of Samburu)

Illustrations by Matthew Hams pp 14 (t), 16, 33, 34, 44, 50, 56 (tr), 72, 73, 86, 105, 155, 159, 162; Alex Hedworth (Eye Candy Illustration) pp 38, 48 (b), 56 (ml), 76, 80, 88, 91 (l), 94, 163; David Russell pp 15, 20, 47, 51, 82, 92, 111; Martin Sanders (Beehive Illustration) pp 21, 41, 62, 64; Laszlo Veres (Beehive Illustration) pp 14 (b), 19, 24, 31, 48 (mr), 49, 55, 63, 67, 79, 81, 83, 91 (r), 95, 99, 103, 115, 164